A NEW SONG

A NEW SONG

Our Journey Toward Healing

SUSAN HABEGGER

ISBN: ISBN: 979-8-9902797-0-4

Cover Design by Mikel Allen, Mikel Allen Designs
Cover Drawing *A New Song* by Glen L. Byrd
Cover Photography by Susan Habegger
Book Design by Mikel Allen, Mikel Allen Designs and Susan Habegger
Book Illustrations by Brandon L. Byrd, Glen L. Byrd, Shiloh W. Byrd

RESPONSES TO *A NEW SONG*

A New Song is not a list of fixes for the troubles of life. It's not a technical manual for psychological healing. It is not just another "YOU CAN DO IT!" for those who are experiencing the trauma of betrayal or loss. Susan Habegger introduces you to the Traveling Companion who has walked with her through crushing loss and has given her tools for moving forward with life. Beautifully written, *A New Song* is a deliberate, intimate, powerful pathway to transposing the heaviness of life in a minor key to the major key of confidence and trust in God.

> Jean Nystrand, Retired Executive Director BSF International,
> Bible Teacher, Thrive Life Skills Board President

A New Song brings freshness and vitality to a timely issue, namely personal suffering. Susan makes suffering more bearable and redemptive. She draws the reader into her own saga with soft, invitational questions. Somehow Susan makes suffering take on a new valence, a new dimension. Dealing with personal suffering can be deceptively simple and daringly hard. This book can be a highly recommendable adventure into our own lives, our own sense of the meaning of our own suffering.

> Dr. Albert Rossi, Clinical Psychologist and Director of Counseling and
> Psychological Services at St. Vladimir's Orthodox Seminary

In *A New Song*, Susan Habegger transparently and innovatively reflects upon the grisly, all-too-present reality of human suffering and personal pain. Through this valuable volume, she bears winsome witness that "suffering produces perseverance; perseverance, character; and character, hope" (Romans 5:3-4) and that "Weeping may last through the night, but joy comes in the morning" (Psalm 30:5). If you or someone you know is struggling with or perhaps drowning in suffering, then this book will prove to be both a salve and a lifeline.

> Todd D. Still, Ph.D., Charles J. and Eleanor McLerran DeLancey Dean and
> William M. Hinson Professor of Christian Scriptures, Baylor University,
> Truett Seminary, Waco, TX USA

Susan's gentle, honest writing offers a sanctuary for the wounded soul and creates a safe space where healing can flourish. She emboldens readers with permission and courage to go into the depths of their hearts and explore places that have long needed tending to. As you travel this road from suffering toward healing through *A New Song*, you have a wise, trusted friend walking the path alongside you.

Denisha Workizer, Founder and Executive Director of Reclaimed Story,
Trauma Survivor

Authentic courage and tender wisdom; we encounter both in Susan Habegger. In her new book, *A New Song*, she writes of a *journey*, because that is what is has been for her, what it always is for those who want to find healing after the experience of trauma. In Christ, suffering and song are not mutually exclusive. I am grateful for her testimony and wisdom. Her readers will be, as well.

Don Guthrie, Pastor First Baptist Church, San Antonio, Texas (retired)

I have been shepherding congregations through seasons of conflict for some 25 years, and trauma (and the church's poor responses to it) have often been at the heart of the conflict. This work is exactly what the church needs to better understand what this journey toward healing should entail. It is Spirit-filled wisdom at its best, and I am so very grateful for it.

Blake Coffee, Executive Director of One Another Project

Susan Habegger, in *A New Song*, invites you to join her on a journey toward wholeness, hope, and peace. With the wisdom that only comes from having "been there done that" through her personal loss and trauma, Susan will gently guide you through your suffering into the wide expanse of healing, freedom, and joy. Take the time to stop and ponder "the bends in the road." In those bends, you will come to better understand what trauma is, its effect on you, who you are, and the nature of God - your traveling companion. This is one journey you won't regret!

Norma Donovan, Founder and president of Restoring Hearts Ministry,
Author of *Restoring Your Heart to Deepen Intimacy*.

A *New Song*'s insights as revealed through Susan Habegger's deep knowledge and understanding of God's compassionate, forgiving, and healing grace opens the heart in a deeply trusting interaction with Him regarding our pain. The result is a profound relief of the pain that has crippled us emotionally and spiritually and now opens us to experience our relationships with greater trust and growing intimacy. Joy and peace replace our pain and anxiety!

Jean Orr, Retired LCSW:Licensed Clinical Social Worker

We all have a story that belongs only to us. Along the way we have incurred disappointment, abuse and trauma. We cannot become the complete person God created us to be without looking at our trauma and allowing the healing process to begin. Susan shows us how to safely walk the journey toward healing, reconciliation, and freedom in order to be free from "what is expected of me." We are not left to walk this hard journey alone. Susan introduces us to our traveling companion, God, who brings us to a place of peace and freedom. Take this journey with honesty and without fear and become the real you . . . God's beautiful masterpiece.

Sally Knipe, Author of *The Do's And Don'ts of Grief*, Ministry to Widows

A *New Song* is a deeply compassionate, highly practical help to anyone who has experienced suffering—no matter the source. With her gentle wisdom and the unmistakable voice of experience, first Susan makes the troublesome topic of suffering approachable. Then she skillfully guides the reader on their own personal journey from despair to hope, from injury to healing, and from the turmoil of being held captive by pain toward freedom, peace and a joyful new song.

Nancy Nelson, Executive Assistant at Reclaimed Story, 34 years in ministry

Welcome to the club that no one wants to join. The solidarity among those who have suffered is a great blessing, but all too often, the road feels lonely difficult to navigate. What if you had a friend with similar experiences, profound spiritual insight, endless patience, an open schedule, and a gift for helping you unravel the complicated tangle of emotions in your heart? This book is the voice of a companion and a coach, a friend who has been there and made it out the other side. This book will help you process and tell your story, and will guide you to healing and peace.

Elissa Bjeletich Davis, Author, Podcaster and Speaker

To my Good Shepherd

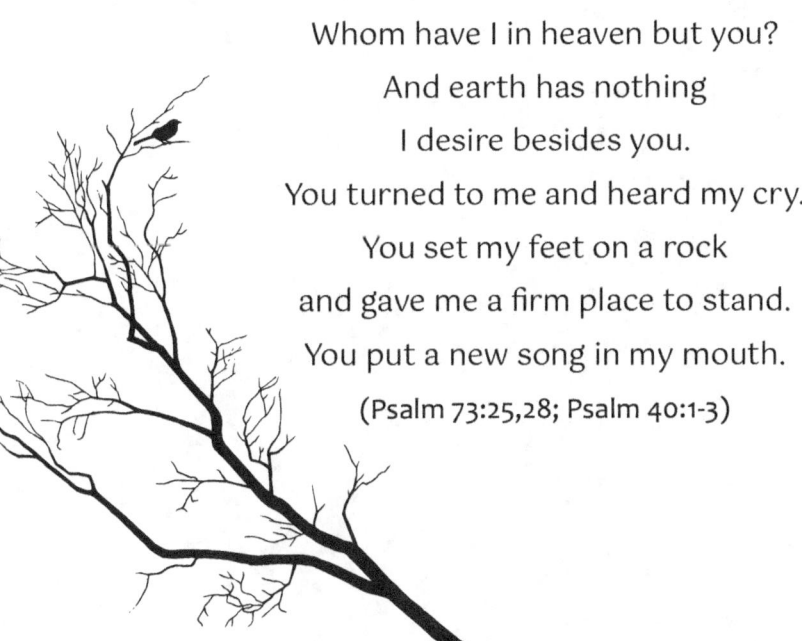

Whom have I in heaven but you?
And earth has nothing
I desire besides you.
You turned to me and heard my cry.
You set my feet on a rock
and gave me a firm place to stand.
You put a new song in my mouth.

(Psalm 73:25,28; Psalm 40:1-3)

CONTENTS

PREFACE

WHERE IT ALL BEGAN

Years before *A New Song* came to life, God planted the international ministry from which it would bloom. After fourteen years of working in multiple countries around the world, including living in Nigeria, I had become intimately acquainted with the multitude of needs in our world. Physical pain. Betrayal. Accusation. Poverty. Marginalization. Abuse. Displacement from home and country.

So many suffered—people with immensely varying traumatic experiences and cultural backgrounds. And yet, their expressions of pain all carried a very similar tune:

"I have no value or purpose."

"How do I respond to the conflict that surrounds me?"

"Where do I belong?"

"How is God different from those who have abused and forsaken me?"

When faced with the reality of others' suffering, those of us who want to help wonder, "What can we do to fix it?" But the solutions we offer in response are often less than helpful. If honestly put into words, they might sound like "They should make their lives look more like mine" or "They should put the suffering in a box—set it aside, forget the past, and just move on."

So, after years of grappling with this question, I felt God fill my mind and heart with the following vision:

We must come alongside those who suffer—in the circumstances
under which they must live their lives. We must give them tools to thrive
where they are
and help them discover hope for a courageous and peaceful way forward.

From this vision, and for this intent, Thrive Life Skills was incorporated in 2010 as a 501(c)(3) charity.[1] God opened doors in Africa, Asia, and Europe for Thrive to come alongside mission organizations, church leadership, community leaders, counselors, and individuals whose hearts were for those living in hurt.

Interacting with many around the world in this capacity, I was no stranger to trauma. But then, in an alarming moment of impact, suffering suddenly became more personal, changing my perspective on how to respond. Through my own healing journey, God compelled me to write material for a training course titled *Moving Forward from Trauma* (updated revision available Fall 2024). This course was designed for mission groups and churches around the world who needed a way to open the conversation about suffering with those just beginning the healing journey. It was intended to answer the call in Psalm 74: 21: "Do not let the oppressed retreat in disgrace; may the poor and needy praise your name."

As I went on the road with that training, first to refugee camps in Thailand and then to several locations in India, I discovered that the time was indeed right for the types of conversations that leaders would learn to facilitate through *Moving Forward from Trauma*—conversations that addressed questions such as these:

"We have suffered for so many years. How do we recover?"

"We have never talked about our suffering. How do we begin?"

"Is there hope? How do we encourage others to share their stories?"

"I do not know how to respond when someone tells me about their pain."

Over time, word spread, and God brought requests from others—Uganda, Nigeria, Ethiopia, and Ukraine. I made return trips to Thailand and India as well. The influx of refugees to the United States from Myanmar brought the work stateside. As *Moving Forward From Trauma* came into the hands of fellow workers, many said, "I want this guidance, too, but in a hands-on form—like a personal journey that I can travel at my own speed and in my own space."

---

[1] For more information about *Thrive Life Skills,* visit thrivelifeskills.com.

Those last words initiated the call. With them, the seeds for *A New Song* were planted.

And now it is here—a companion for all those on the personal journey of healing. It intends to answer the call of Psalm 40:1–3 (emphasis mine):

> I waited patiently for the LORD;
> he turned to me and heard my cry
> he set my feet on a rock and gave me a firm place to stand.
> *He put a new song in my mouth*, a hymn of praise to our God.

This book shows us that, in our suffering, we often cannot see the "beyond" that is waiting. Rather, it is as we take each next step that God puts in front of us that the journey comes to life. In some places, the path might feel uncomfortable, unfamiliar, or downright perilous; while in other places, we clearly see evidence of *good* and *beauty*. But above the bad and good, and above all the chaos that seems to swirl around, we trust the God who is ALL. We listen for the voice of our Good Shepherd, who is with us in our suffering—and as we do, we find the narrative of our story unfolding, with purpose and value.

As the writing of *A New Song* neared completion, it was read and used by pre-release small groups, and the response was remarkable. It brought to light the number of people who need a defined way to begin the conversation about hurt and healing and may want to do so in community.

For those who want to use *A New Song* as a group study, *A NEW SONG LEADERS GUIDE FOR SMALL GROUP STUDY* is also available.

THANK YOU

I have been thinking about this portion of the book since I began the manuscript. Perhaps, it is because I have been so vividly aware of how others have poured into this effort in so many ways. To those of you who have, you may not realize how God used your words and actions to reassure me of this call to write—to say to my spirit, "Keep going." As one friend expressed it, "Press on, dear sister, press on."

First, thank you to those who requested that I write a book such as this. Responding to my teaching on trauma, you said, "I want similar information and thoughts in a hands-on form, so I can make this a personal journey that I can travel at my own speed and in my own space." Your words initiated the call.

The opportunity for teaching and for writing this book grew out of my work with Thrive Life Skills. You can read more about this connection in the backstory for this book, which appears in the Preface. Jean Nystrand, Holly Kennedy, Duane Kiihne (deceased September 2023), Linda Musfeldt, Ron Reaoch, Tom Skaff, and Patty Yoss, thank you! Your friendship and counsel as my board members are a blessing to me. You have wisely advised me over the years, and when this opportunity came, you encouraged me to take what was created for international use and adapt it for further effectiveness in this new format. God brought each of you to me for particular reasons, and I can't imagine A New Song or Thrive without you.

I'm not sure that editors are always mentioned in this section of the book, but Lynn Everett, you are a gift to this work. You brilliantly made the necessary corrections; and far beyond that, you connected with the heart of the message, editing in ways that not only helped the words flow more smoothly but also held true to my intentions. We have both mentioned God's hand in bringing us together. I look forward to more projects with you.

In 2018, Mikel Allen sent an email to me after I moved from San Antonio: "We miss you! Let us know if there is ANYTHING we can do to help you." God reminded me of that email in late 2023—and so, I did just that. Mikel, thank you for your formatting and design work and for your patience with me as I moved this here and that there, tweaking this color and that font. Thank you for believing in this project that God put on my heart and for seeing it as a call to *you* as well.

Thank you to the women of St. Luke Christian Orthodox Church in Erie, Colorado, who announced, "We are having a workshop about suffering—everyone come!" And to the many who came, committing to a twelve-week workshop based on an early draft of *A New Song*, thank you for being gracious and opening your hearts and voices to share your stories in a new way. Thank you, Margaret and Frances, for leading with me. You all helped bring life to the words and validated the heart and intention of *A New Song*.

Among those wonderful coincidences that were, in fact, God-circumstances was the lunch with high school friends where Rhonda Sprunger said, "You need to connect with my good friend, Denisha." That pronouncement introduced a relationship between two organizations and a group of women who strengthened one another and were destined to work together. Thank you, Rhonda!

Denisha Workizer (founder and director) and Nancy Nelson (executive assistant) of *Reclaimed Story*, thank you for your companionship, personally and in ministry. You are an unexpected but much-longed-for gift from God. I value our like-mindedness and the way we nudge each other forward onto new ideas and opportunities. You breathed courage into the experience and added practical advice and next steps to my ideas. Thank you for being a major cheer club for the completion and publication of this book. Your words of encouragement still ring assuredly in my ears.

Thank you to the leaders and participants of *A New Song* life groups through *Reclaimed Story*. Using drafts and watermarked pages of the book sessions that were emailed to you each week, you took the journey. You are a blessing to me. Your commitment spoke to me of the need for such a book study, and your responses of healing and gratitude during the final stages of publication came at just the right moment.

The assignment to find those who will not only read the manuscript but also potentially endorse it is a daunting and humbling task. Thank you to Blake Coffee, Elissa Bjeletich Davis, Norma Donovan, Don Guthrie, Sally Knipe, Nancy Nelson, Jean Nystrand, Jean Orr, Dr. Albert Rossi, Dr. Todd Still, and Denisha Workizer for graciously responding, "Yes!" You encouraged me with your attention and time and amazed me in the ways that you caught the heart of the work in your own words.

When a friendship strengthens over multiple international trips, you know it is a good one. Sue Nelson, thank you for our northern Uganda adventures. You sat through many teaching sessions and encouraged me forward with your reassurance that having the message in book form was important. I thank God for you.

There are also those who contributed to the book by the way they cared for me along my own journey. Kristi and Mike, you stayed by me through the ups and the downs. You experienced the "Susan" on the pages of this book. You listened, helped me dream again, spoke words to help me rebuild confidence, cried and laughed with me. You watched this work come to life out of the everyday bends in the road. Thank you for walking this journey with me.

When I needed dedicated writing time, Aunt Carol, thank you for welcoming me into your home—and for protected quiet hours, sustenance waiting for me at lunch, a listening ear, and Rummikub games in the evenings. Those moments are part of the structure and strength of this book. Your love and care are a part of who I am as a writer.

Some friends are in it for the long haul. Vivian Haney, our friendship began in sixth grade, and many years later, when I called from across the country with news that my life as I knew it was shattered, your response was, "I'm coming." You walked the bends in the road with me, even up to the final months of the book's completion. You read chapters, asked questions, and gave suggestions. And you assured me that this project is on your heart in a special way. God has used your commitment to encourage me forward. Thank you, friend. Here's to many more years.

It is always good to have a big brother on your side. Ron and Cheryl, you encouraged me that mom and dad would be happy with this endeavor and told me to keep going. Thank you for loving me through it all.

I live with my daughter, son-in-law, and five grandchildren. Thank you, dear family, for allowing me to do life with you, so that I can give my full time to this work. You have been gracious, kind, and patient with me, often answering "What does your grandmother do?" with "She helps people talk about their pain." Thank you for understanding what I do and for joining me in that calling. From our little chats early in the morning to decisions about word choices and colors and spacing—your opinions mattered. Thank you for reminding me of truth when I faltered and doubted myself. Thank you for walks on the beach and to the forest—opportunities to clear my mind, to laugh, and to enjoy God's beauty.

To my son-in-law, Brandon, and my grandsons, Glen and Shiloh, thank you for sharing your gift of art and creativity with me—and others—through the illustrations in the book and on the cover. You grasped the concepts I described in words and brought them to life in pencil, watercolor, and pastels. Your contributions add visual meaning to difficult concepts and express beauty that is so needed as we find our way through healing.

And to my Good Shepherd, my perfect Traveling Companion—my heart is full of gratitude. You have mercifully rescued me at times when I stumbled and stepped outside the protective boundaries you lovingly gave me. You brought calm, peace, and reassurance when the unexpected storms raged about me and I feared I would drown. You set my feet on a rock and gave me a new song. You are my ALL.

Dear traveler,

Even though I don't know your story, I want you to know that I feel connected to you.

I am very much aware that our faithful Traveling Companion, our Creator, knows both of us, and so, in some way—maybe through this book or through our shared human experience of pain, or both—He is connecting us.

Like you, I am no stranger to suffering. In fact, I have been "living" this book for many years, often writing chapters "in the moment"— sometimes after a traumatic incident, other times upon gaining a newfound awareness of pain. During these times, my words would come: "Oh, God, I don't want to feel this, and I don't know what to do with it!" And I would hear His clear response: *"Write it down. There is another whom I love, who needs to hear this and know they are not alone."*

And now you are here: that *"another"* is you.

I am a visual person, and so I have sometimes pictured you holding this book in your hand, sitting with it in a quiet place, or setting it on the table beside your bed or chair. In the process, I have come to envision it as a companion for your journey—one that can lead you through the uncertainty, out of the numbness, and toward healing.

You alone will decide how closely to hold to this companion. You may be happy just to make its acquaintance—skimming through pages, picking up a thought or two—or you may find it a trusted friend with whom you can settle in for the long haul. But you might bear in mind just a few simple things as you make your decision.

First, know that the chapters are ordered to follow a continuous thought process, with each chapter building on previous ones; so, I recommend starting at the beginning and following it through.

Also, some chapters are longer and more intense than others, so don't be discouraged if you are in a chapter that feels like "too much." Moments of respite—visuals, short poems, or other light reading—are deliberately sprinkled into the mix, just when you might need encouragement. Many chapters also end with "A Bend in the Road," a short section that offers you time to be still and contemplate any new awareness or pending decision you may be facing. I encourage you not to pass over these sections—but don't force them either. If you aren't ready for a particular bend in the road, make a note, continue on, and circle back around later. Your strength and courage will grow slowly by slowly, and soon you will be able to return.

Finally, this book is not a project to complete and add to the shelf. There is no need to rush through to "the end." Your journey will be ever-unfolding, which means that even beyond the final pages of this book, your path may lead you back—to revisit a chapter, add to a bend in the road, or uncover a new layer.

So, you decide. *A New Song* will be here, in whatever capacity you need, as a companion on your journey through suffering.

I am here too. And our Traveling Companion, who knows us both, will never stop coming alongside.

Thoughtfully Yours,

Susan

PREPARATION FOR THE JOURNEY

Perhaps, one of the most precious gifts we can receive in suffering is a quiet and safe place for the journey.

SO MANY STORIES

Every person has a story.
Every story is unique,
   made of delicately stitched details
     woven in and out
     with threads of
      pain,
        joy,
          suffering,
          comfort.

Most stories are never spoken:
unexpressed in human language,
never heard by human ears.

Yet, all are valuable.
All are known.
Treasured
   and recorded
     by God.

When Naomi told her story, she didn't wrap it up in a pretty package. She didn't pretend to have answers for her pain. Instead, she delivered it with honest emotion and truthful words. She opened her heart and let it spill forth.

Her story, told in the biblical book of Ruth, is one of sadness and loss. It starts with fearing starvation for her family and then being obliged to her husband's decision to flee to a foreign land. Packing up and leaving everything behind— their family, friends, community, and culture—they travel with two small sons and set up a new home in a hostile environment. Later she becomes a widow. And in time, she experiences the death of both sons.

Afflicted. Alone. Apprehensive. These words come to describe her new identity. Left on her own, Naomi goes back to her homeland. And there, she tells her story.

> "Don't call me Naomi," she told them. "Call me Mara, because the Almighty has made my life very bitter. I went away full, but the LORD has brought me back empty." (Ruth 1:20)

Naomi spoke the raw truth about her pain and emotions. Essentially she was saying:

> "My loss leaves me feeling empty."

> "The events of my life taste bitter to me."

> "I feel afflicted, burdened."

> "I remember how I used to feel and now that blessing is gone."

I connect with Naomi. I have also experienced suffering as part of my story. If I am to be honest, as Naomi was, I, too, tasted only bitterness for a time. I was empty. The blessing was gone. *I thought I would never sing with joy again.*

Maybe you have felt that way. Maybe you feel that way today. Life tastes bitter. Emptiness invades each day. The despair is tangible. You have lost your "song."

Listen to these words from Psalm 40:1-3, written by a man named David about his own story:

> I waited patiently for the LORD;
> he turned to me and heard my cry
> he set my feet on a rock and gave me a firm place to stand.
> *He put a new song in my mouth*, a hymn of praise to our God.

I connect with David too. I now also have a new song.

This new song is different from the one I used to sing. It comes from deep within. In fact, it is rooted in the soil of suffering. It rises out of the pain and is filled with the expression of my gratitude to God that He is with me in my suffering. That He heard my cry. That He set my feet on a rock. That there is sweetness once again in my life.

That *He* put a new song in my mouth.

We later discover that this new song becomes part of Naomi's journey as well—as provision, peace, and even joy reenter her story.

This is the reality and it is the foundation for our journey. Without this possibility, we are left to falter. Left to merely survive, when what we desperately long for is to sing again.

If you have experienced deep suffering, you might not see any potential to express a new song. You may not think a happy ending to your story is possible. Naomi and David and I would tell you that there are no quick and easy answers; there is no positive facade that you should wear, no special words that you should say. But there is a way forward, through the darkness, out of the numbness.

It may take time, but it is an honest journey on a path of healing. So, if you are weary of the pain, I invite you to join us.

3
" . . . I MUST WALK IT ALONE."

One evening as my mother and I sat in quietness, she said gently, but matter-of-factly, "There is a path ahead of me . . . and I must walk it alone."

At 46, I had recently returned from living overseas. And now, my mother had ovarian cancer. It came to light, *accidentally*, through surgery for an unrelated reason. She and my father discussed the options and results of possible treatment. They settled on comfort from pain and hospice care. No chemotherapy. No radiation. No surgery. There was a sad, yet certain peace in this decision for all of us.

My father, brother, and I came alongside to walk the journey with her. Together, we talked, we prayed, we cried. We discussed options for care and pain relief. We planned for the shortened future that remained. We were involved in every possible way.

But, my mother's statement that night was profound and clear: "I must walk it alone."

> My mother knew, however, that she was never completely alone. She enjoyed the presence of a traveling companion—her loving and perfect Creator, who had walked with her without fail on every part of her journey to this point in time. She knew that He would be with her through every unexpected change, every experience of pain, every moment of doubt. So, when my mother said *alone*, she meant: "*with my companion*."

Still, our hearts ached. We would have done anything for her in order to lighten the burden for her. But there was only so much we could do. The essence of the journey was my mother's task. *She* had to accept the reality of the disease within her own body. *She* had to learn to live at peace with the unseen enemy that was slowly destroying her physical identity.

She had to experience the changes that this traumatic illness brought to every part of her physical, emotional, and spiritual being.

She had to adjust her perspective from years to months to days to hours; and she had to balance hope, reality, sorrow, and joy.

Then, there was the actual step-by-step walk through the valley of the shadow of death—my mother had to traverse the path that bridges this world to the next. That invisible final transition from what *was* to what *would be*. As much as we wanted to carry some of that burden, to help clarify the uncertainty, *she* was the one who would take the journey. We were not. She recognized this reality, and she took on the task with determination and intentionality.

The path of emotional healing is much the same.

We certainly do not need a crowd of people on that path with us. At first, we might think we want company; but the noisy advice, the unintentional accusations, and the insistent call to joy often become more than we can handle.

One or two may come alongside, and we are grateful for their presence. We can absorb courage from the few who walk with us, offering a hand and simply sharing space with us.

Yet, that invisible transition from what *was* to what *will be*—we must traverse that part alone. No one can heal *for us*. As much as others want to absorb the pain, the journey is personal. It is *our* story.

In my mother's case, she was facing departure from this world—the world she knew. There would be a clear ending to what *had been*, and there would be no way for her to carry it into *what would be*. The path she had to walk took her through death and into new life.

In many ways, healing from suffering is also a journey of death. It must be.

The difficulty with this journey comes because our first reaction is to *preserve life*. At most times, this instinct serves us well. But when it comes to emotional trauma and suffering, this instinct can act as a trap. It causes us to hold onto what "was"—or what we *thought* "was" or what we wanted to believe "was." We attempt to breathe life back into that *remembered* or *imagined* picture once again.

But the reality is that we cannot restore that picture to its former glory. The picture has been broken, and the pieces we are left with will never fit back together precisely as they once did. Some are chipped, and there are new pieces as well—truths that we did not see before. Yet we cannot "un-see" what we have now seen. We cannot "un-know" what we now know.

And as long as we try to build new life around diseased events, we cannot heal. The poison continues to infect.

Our instinct to preserve life and avoid loss, however, remains. Therefore, along our contemplative journey, we will talk more about how to identify this sense of loss within ourselves. We will also discover how to mourn it in ways that are healthy and beneficial, rather than destructive. For now, it is simply time to absorb the reality that *life, as you knew it*—or *as you hoped it would be or believed it to be*—*is changed*.

Perhaps, you are faced with pain from a recent event. Or it may be that suffering from long ago continues to appear, uninvited, into the foreground. Your suffering might also be due to a growing awareness of an ongoing struggle. This could be a broken or hurtful relationship, a health challenge, or a difficult work situation. Or you might not be sure of the source; you are simply aware of disquiet, of anxiousness, of unsettledness—a sense of apprehension or uneasiness. The presence of pain in each life is personal, unique, and profoundly real. The result, however, is the same: your life has changed.

And this time, the pain is not caused by a sad story about a stranger on the news, or even one about a good friend or family member. It is not possible to just say a few kind words and walk away. This time, it is *your* story. It is personal. There may be some who care and mourn with you. But they cannot feel the presence of the unseen enemy that threatens to slowly destroy your identity. Only you can feel the subtle, yet powerful, impact on every part of your physical, emotional, and spiritual being. Only you are walking this path from what *was* to what *will be.*

Even in your aloneness, there is a Mystery that hovers about, intangible and sometimes unspeakable. It is the One who values your story and has protected it before any of the days of it even came to be.

Perhaps you are not ready to acknowledge Him. Perhaps you are not ready for your conversation with Him. Take your time. He is patient.

If or when you are ready to include Him, you will find that He is full of compassion and totally trustworthy—a valuable companion.

A DIFFERENT KIND OF JOURNEY

Movement. Almost constant movement.

Coming from one place . . . traveling to another.

Like Naomi, like David, like my mother, we are often *on the way.*

Dreaming. Planning.

For what is to come, for what could be,

For what should be, for what we hope will be.

Journeys are an integral part of our lives.

Most often, a journey is considered important primarily because it is the process by which we get *to the destination.* Consequently, we choose the most direct and time-efficient route. Ready to put the travel experience behind us, we race toward the finish line.

- We do not easily embrace the moment and *stay for some time.*
- We fall into the habit of accomplishment, performance, and completion.
- We tend to avoid any implication that we might be going *backward* or that we do not *have it all together.*
- We try to sidestep discomfort and unfamiliarity.
- We steer clear of the formidable *bends in the road.*

No more.

On this journey we are taking together, we are ready to step off the well-worn path of "getting on with life." *We are ready for a different kind of journey.*

This journey gently encourages us to slow down,
    does not require performance,
        provides us a safe place to experience discomfort,
      and gives us permission to speak and listen
          without an immediate need for answers.

This journey does not lead to a finish line. It inspires us toward courage and peace and a profound knowing of ourselves along the way.

6
A CONTEMPLATIVE JOURNEY

Our journey includes action and movement from place to place. The essence of this journey takes place in our thinking, our emotions, and even the intents of our hearts. For this reason, we can describe the journey as *contemplative*.

To *contemplate*. What comes to mind? What image grows?

> To think deeply
>> To consider carefully
>>> To focus one's thoughts on
>>>> To reflect on
>>>> To ponder

Tucked away within each of these ideas is the expectation of . . .

>>>> Unhurried time
>>> Setting aside of all distraction
>> Vulnerability
> Attentiveness
Single-mindedness

Ours will be a *contemplative* journey in the sense that it includes all of the above.

The journey through suffering toward healing is not a journey of quick steps, comparative progress, or rushed restoration. Thinking about it as *contemplative* can help us to slow down, give us direction, and remind us to breathe.

After all, one does not contemplate *quickly*. One also does not contemplate while watching a movie or talking on the phone.

Perhaps, as you think about what it means to take a contemplative path, you feel that contemplation is not productive. Yet consider that it does take effort. Thinking about contemplation also often generates an image of peace; and yet, as we will see, quiet contemplation can sometimes be disturbing and unsettling. Contemplation, then, is taking time to quiet our minds and our actions, intentionally making room for careful, productive thought about things that we might otherwise push aside.

Think of contemplative time as an opportunity to "clear away the clutter" with purpose. Some people like to be organized. They clear away clutter because they like the look and feel of orderliness. They are happy with unused empty space because it allows them the freedom to use that space however they need, whenever they need—to complete a project, for example.

Likewise, we must *clear some clutter* so that we have the space to think and move and do what we need to do more freely. Things such as . . .

> undistracted thinking,
>
> unhurried pondering,
>
> attentive reflection.

The very idea of clearing away all distraction might feel threatening. Televisions, radios, phones, computers, and books provide endless interminable background noise to "protect" us from such attentive reflection.

Virtually every fragment of our daily routines compels us toward activity and response. Every task and every opportunity for input persuades us of its immediate importance to our well-being and our productivity.

As such, a contemplative path feels, in many ways, unnatural. It is not built into the calendar. It is not built into our schedule. And we feel we are too busy being productive to accommodate it. We are too busy adding to the files of information in our minds. Too busy de-stressing through our use of alternative distractions and noise. Too busy getting on with life.

And so, life does go on . . .

> but your story is left untold,
>
> even to you.
>
> *Especially to you.*

Perhaps, you have convinced yourself that your story doesn't matter, because everyone has a story, and everyone's story carries some essence of suffering and pain. Or maybe you think of your own pain comparatively ("My experience is not as bad as hers") or believe that too much time has passed since a hurtful event ("It must no longer be relevant"). So, you have set it aside and convinced yourself that "this is just life; let's get on with it."

These responses might seem logical. They might even feel like the healthy way to deal with pain. Yet, each one demeans and devalues the expression of your story. They all lead us down one path—the setting aside of hurt, of suffering—which ultimately, does not lead to healing, only to deeper pain.

It might be that well-intentioned people have tried to help you in your suffering by attempting to provide in some way—with a new job, a new relationship, or financial stability—something to turn the old to new, the bad to good. Such provision can be helpful; there are legitimate needs to be met. Yet, the underlying message is still the rushed expectation to *return to normalcy*.

Again, this response to suffering presses it down out of sight; but it does not disappear. It only puts on a mask until a moment when it resurfaces unexpectedly and perhaps with more intensity. Our own quick responses and others' expectations oblige us to move quickly forward.

Perhaps, one of the most precious gifts you can receive in suffering is a quiet and safe place for the journey. No expectations, except truth—and even that may come in layers. No promises, except that your story will be heard.

Undistracted thinking. Unhurried pondering. Attentive reflection. One would almost think you are in no hurry to get to the destination. And there is the treasure. *The value of the journey is the journey itself.* This *contemplative journey* is a gift to you.

7

ETIQUETTE FOR THE JOURNEY

A person's story is a valuable possession; to share it with someone is an act of trust. The response we receive to that act of trust is crucial in the healing process, either encouraging or hindering it.

Most of us have had the experience of sharing a part of our story with someone, only to be ridiculed, accused, or ignored. Such negative responses impose feelings of guilt and reinforce the already looming sense within us that we lack value. We often quickly react to them by closing up all of the windows and doors on our heart, determining never to be so foolishly vulnerable again.

For this reason, there is usually a code of behavior—*etiquette*—in spaces where personal stories and details are shared with each other. In a group-sharing situation, for example, the code of behavior, whether formal or unspoken, often includes words such as . . .

Respect

Patience

Compassion

Trust

Truth

Even though your journey may not include interacting with a group of people, it will be important for you to use similar etiquette as you interact with yourself and care for *your own* story as the valuable possession that it is.

Just as you would get to know others in a group through their sharing, you will get to know yourself. There will be times that you like what you see; you will "recognize" and feel comfortable with that person (whether yourself or another) based on what is shared. There will be other times when you are surprised, even shocked, by what is expressed or felt, even when it is in your own words or in your own heart. When that happens, how will you respond?

Let's begin with *respect*.

At all times, *show respect for yourself.* Treat yourself with the same honor that you would extend to another who was sharing their story. An honest "story-telling" is ragged and often, uninviting. Yet, we show respect to the storyteller by being attentive. In the same way, no matter what comes, listen carefully to yourself. Don't turn away when the picture isn't pretty.

Show respect also by shutting out distractions. Have you ever tried to share your personal thoughts with someone, only to realize that person is preoccupied with other things? As you would for another, set aside time for yourself that is protected. Give time and full attention to yourself. You and your story are valuable.

Next, be *patient*.

It is likely that your pain has been growing for months or even years, so it will not be resolved overnight. Do not start your journey by drawing a finish line. Allow yourself to take a slow pace, rather than measuring success by your progress. Don't be discouraged when an emotion that you thought you had conquered sweeps over you unexpectedly. Don't feel guilty when you must retrace some of your steps. Don't give into defeat when, in that process of retracing, you discover more layers of pain. Instead, it is necessary to wait quietly for yourself.

As you travel this contemplative path, you will sometimes experience moments of comprehension—some have called them lightbulb moments or aha moments. At other times, you will face unexpected, even unwanted, moments. Shock. Accusation. New truth. In these moments, hold onto your patience. Allow yourself to feel all of the emotions but avoid overreacting. Allow yourself to see all of the truth but avoid making sweeping judgments. The hills and the valleys, the bends and the turns— they are all necessary parts of the entire journey. *Patiently, take them all in.*

Have *compassion*.

Let's clarify the meaning of compassion. Compassion is not pity. Nor is it unreasonable indulgence. Neither of these things would be helpful or healthful for us. Compassion *does* show itself as deep concern and care for the pain that is being expressed. Real compassion opens the door for sharing and provides a safe place for honest expression of emotion.

So, think carefully about the words that you say to yourself. Are they kind? Are they accusatory? Are they echoes of what you have heard others say to you? Is it always necessary to speak? Are you able to compassionately listen to yourself without an immediate reactionary response or call to action?

Now, *trust* yourself enough to be honest.

As you consider your own role in your story, you might feel the temptation to hide, to deny the rawness of what comes to the surface. I encourage you not to give into this temptation. Do not pretend or play a part. The journey will be wasted if you base your next steps on what you could have or should have done, rather than on what really occurred. There will be no real healing if you put on a face that you think will be more pleasing to others or even to yourself. There will be no resolution if you craft responses as if you were scripting a play.

Hold onto *the combination of compassion and trust*. Woven together, they will create a strong anchor that will steady you and keep you from being swept away by the waves of regret—by the could haves and should haves that are unwelcome on this journey. We will put them in their proper place as time goes on.

Finally, commit to *truth*.

Speak truth not only about yourself. Speak truth about others. Speak truth about events. Speak truth about the evil and about your response to the evil.

Sometimes the truth will bring an immediate sense of freedom. Sometimes it will sting. But always, truth will move you in the right direction. Your instinct might tell you that hiding the truth will protect you from pain or that embellishing the truth will give you opportunity to defend yourself. But truth—real truth—even with its jagged edges, will always move you further from captivity and closer to healing.

In some instances, as you honestly peel back the layers of a particular truth, you may reveal new details and discover new truth. If this happens, don't be afraid to correct the narrative. This takes courage. But it will serve you well on your journey of healing. There will be no real healing if you rewrite the story dishonestly. So, in all things, speak truth.

Respect. Patience. Compassion. Trust. Truth.

Most of us assume that we know ourselves. And many of us may. However, we always get to know someone more intimately when we go on a journey with them. By being your own companion on this journey, you will get to know yourself more. As you do, you will begin to discover what healing looks like and feels like for *you*. Your path of suffering is not the same as anyone else's; and your new song will not have the same melody as another's. So, you should never expect to fit your expression of healing into a preconceived checklist of accomplishments.

At times, the path will feel bright and welcoming. You will feel courageous and ready for newness. At other times, it will be difficult to see through the darkness and the clouds. Parts of the journey will be frightening, even threatening. Other stretches of the path will be encouraging and full of hope. In the midst of it all, the intention is for you to feel safe, to be heard, and to become aware that you are *seen, known, and loved*.

As such, this contemplative journey is to be a protected place. So, be careful about sharing too much with others. Such protective carefulness will flow from your respect and compassion for yourself. Think again about what it means to take this journey. Gather the precious moments of your story and ponder them in your heart. As you give them time and energy, they will grow in value and clarity, and an intriguing, yet undeniable, confidence will emerge. As that confidence increases, you will come to discern how and when to share with others.

Be a good companion to yourself. And if the path ever seems desolate for a moment, know that you are never completely alone.

8

BENDS IN THE ROAD

When I'm traveling an unfamiliar highway, I do not like to be caught behind a large truck that impedes my view. I feel stressed, unsure of the turns and bends that may suddenly appear. I want to see the road in front of me. I want to be aware of any impending need for caution.

When a sharp bend in the road does appear in front of me, I know it is time to take it slowly. The turn itself may cause trouble if taken at great speed. It is also wise to slow down to observe what challenges and changes may await on the other side of the bend.

For these reasons, at various times on our contemplative journey, I will advise you whenever we are about to come to *"a bend in the road."*

This will help you to know that a time of *slowing down* and contemplation is ahead.

A time to focus on a particular challenge of the journey.

A time to think carefully and observe the landscape, so that you can prepare for any new encounters that may lie on the other side.

Every bend will permit, even encourage, careful consideration related to some part of our relationship with suffering; as such, a separate section that includes a journaling activity will be devoted to each. These pages will be titled "A Bend In The Road." They are hands-on and visual, and they invite your expression and participation.

These bends in the road are not intended to be threats or stumbling blocks. Rather, they are meant to allow you time for contemplation and space to step out of the "what is expected of me" mindset. They offer you a safe place to pause and consider the various chapters of your story.

These bends in the road will bring clarity along the path. Each will hold an opportunity for courage and for peace.

Be assured as you watch the road ahead . . .

I will let you know they are coming.

BEGINNING THE STORY

*Your story is not confined to
one moment in time.*

*Every event, the positive and the negative,
has value and
is a significant part of your story.*

9

HOW DO WE BEGIN?

Telling your story . . . how did you imagine it would feel?

The telling of our story actually begins within. Before we can express it to anyone else, we must speak it truthfully to ourselves.

And so, the first task is to sit quietly with *yourself*. For hours, perhaps. Or over a period of days. Begin to feel comfortable with *you*—for *you* are your closest traveling companion on this journey.

Then, when you are ready, you will want to express your story so that it is heard, even if only by you. What will that look like?

When prompted to tell about our lives, we usually respond in one of two ways:

One response is to begin with a list of experiences—dates on the calendar, accomplishments, failures, moments of fear, moments of joy—one after another. The ups and downs, with some events that last for days and others for just a few moments.

Yet, the reality is that your story is more than just individual events. There is a tapestry that weaves through and around and between each event. Life is a story, and sometimes, the "between the event" times are just as descriptive of the story. These are the moments of response and adjustment to change. We will learn more about these parts of the journey as we travel on.

A second response is to define life with one sweeping declaration: "My life has been bad," or "My life has been good." Or maybe even, "My life has been full of sorrow" or "My life has been unfair."

But, once again, the narrative of life is more than one statement. It is more than one chapter of the story.

Suppose you are looking at a forest of trees. An artist asks you to describe what you see so she can paint the image on canvas. You say, "The trees are green." There is a certain amount of truth to that answer; but if you look more carefully, you will discover shades of color. "Green" does not completely, or even correctly, describe the entire forest. There is more to the image than one simple word or descriptive phrase could cover.

And so it is with your life. It is more than "good" or "bad" or even "full of sorrow." There are shades of "good" *and* "bad"; there are variations of "sorrow" and even "happiness."

Perhaps, in your life, one event seems to consume the story. Maybe it happened many months or years ago or perhaps you are still in the midst of it. Regardless, it feels like that event has taken over your life, and nothing else has survived. So, when you think about your story, you describe it in the same way that you would describe only that one event; the situation seems to be the description for *all of life*.

For these reasons, we often need help in getting started.

The word *narrative* is a good place to start. A *narrative* is a written or spoken account of connected events. It is like that forest full of trees. At first glance, all we see is a group of individual trees, and they *do* all look green—but if we step back, clear our eyes, and refocus our gaze with more intention, we begin to differentiate the various hues, along with the lights and shadows, that make up the "green." And we begin to see how individual trees overlap and intertwine.

Likewise, the narrative of your life is complicated and detailed. But, right now, as you take your first look at it, only certain aspects may be visible. The trees may all appear to be green. That is okay; we'll start *there*.

Let's identify what is most visible right now; we'll begin with a sketch of a few ups and down in your life. The details and nuances will come later. Yes, this is our first bend in the road—at the very beginning.

A BEND IN THE ROAD

HOW DO WE BEGIN?

On the next page, turn your book so that you can draw a line lengthwise in the empty space. This gives you more room for your timeline. Add a mark at the beginning of the line; this is when you were born. Add another mark at the end of the line; that mark is "today."
This line represents your entire existence.

Now, it's time to add a few experiences. Don't allow this to be overwhelming. We are simply *beginning* your story. Start with a positive experience. Identify this positive event ABOVE the line, using just a few words. Place it on the timeline at a point that shows approximately when it happened in your life—for example, early on, in the middle, or recently.

Next do the same with a negative event. Identify the event BELOW the line, also just in a few words and in a place that indicates when in your life it happened.

Now, add two or three more of each type of experience, positive and negative. When you are finished, your timeline might look something like this:

As you consider what experiences to add, don't measure the significance of any one event based on what other people see. For example, an experience might be just a small moment in time that profoundly impressed upon your memory; for that, it merits words on the page. Later, if you think of other events that are equally or more significant than the ones you've already listed, you may decide to return to this page and add them.

Finally, avoid getting sidetracked by the details and emotions of each situation that you write down. The purpose of this exercise is to help you simply to begin to visualize your story, including the ups and the downs, the positives and the negatives. The time for pondering these events in detail will come later.

YOUR TIMELINE:

Contemplate for a Moment

When you are finished writing down your experiences, take a look at your timeline. It speaks to just a fraction of all that has happened in your life. If you added other events, both positive and negative, you could expand the line. And if you were to tell the entire story of your life, this line would be very long indeed!

Each experience adds to your story, but it's not just about taking up more space on a timeline; every experience, positive and negative, has—and adds—value and significance in your life. In other words, your time on this earth has not been insignificant or unimportant. Your story might be unknown to others, but that does not mean it is without value.

In our journey together, although you will focus on particular moments in your life, it will be important to see that your story is not confined to one moment in time or a single circumstance; it will be important to see that your story is not even confined to a mere series of events on a timeline. Rather, you must see the enormous reality of your life.

Look at your timeline. Envision it expanded, full of events, wrapped in emotions. You might even look up into the sky and picture it stretched across the heavens. Give it life, allow it to be more than just a description of individual moments in time.

Breathe deeply and begin to accept the vastness of this story—your story.

Ponder the following truth until you begin to believe it, and then write it next to your timeline:

Every event, spoken or unspoken, is significant.

Every moment, positive or negative, is important.

This life—my life—is valuable.

Maybe you will come to a place where you believe that truth today—or it may be another day. Be patient with yourself. This is part of the journey. Be courageous.

Your story is not coincidental or random.

Your story is not a series of chaotic events.

Your story is not in the hands of others.

It is not without purpose,

      is not insignificant,

      is not a mistake.

Your story is unique,

      has value,

        expresses beauty.

Your story is yours,

      and it is not done.

Known and recorded,

your story is more than a series of events.

It is protected by the One Who set it in place,

    held close and treasured by the One who loves you perfectly—

    the One who walks this journey with you.

> Keep me as the apple of your eye;
> hide me in the shadow of your wings…
> (Psalm 17:8)

The story begins, and we become fully aware that, without invitation or even permission, suffering plays a significant part in the narrative.

There is a moment of impact.

It is A moment that quite literally shakes us and destroys the foundation on which we stand. It might be an event or a flash of realization. It might be the understanding of an emotion that has been plaguing us. But it is as if a carpet has been pulled out from underneath—we lose our footing, and we are sent spinning into the unknown.

A moment of crisis.

We *feel* what has happened. We experience it physically or emotionally or both; but clearly, we know that something has changed. It is difficult to describe the sensations. The sounds around us may seem muted—or painfully loud. General day-to-day activity seems almost annoying. Why is life continuing on as if nothing has happened? Even the air we breathe feels a bit strange.

However we script it, images and emotions like *danger*, *disbelief*, *fear*, and *panic* enter our story. In a very real way, life, as we have known it, *stops*.

This is the crisis moment. The moment we are forced to see some part of our lives in a new way—a new way that is a threat to our well-being.

You can see it here, in the image. The crisis is a moment that sends shards flying.

- It makes a mark that cannot be erased.

- It grabs our attention.

- From that moment on, it attempts to consume us.

Whether our crisis is visible (a shocking event witnessed by others) or invisible (perhaps to those who know us, our lives look as if nothing has changed), a new awareness takes hold . . . of old pain, of new pain, or of ongoing pain that we thought would have come to a close by now.

Even if others don't know what has happened, *we feel the impact.* We are troubled by what has happened. Deep inside, confusion and unrest are taking over.

Suffering has entered our story.

Take a deep breath.

I have heard that phrase at various points in my life.

At times, I have spoken it to myself . . .
    before making a significant decision,
    before a much-anticipated event,
    before a moment of intense physical pain,
    before responding in anger or frustration,
    before speaking into a stressful situation,
    Even before doing something that I love.

    Before walking away from
           or running toward.

    Before jumping into
          a cold lake,
          place of responsibility,
          a relationship,
          a new venture.

    Before collapsing into
          confusion,
          fear,
          despair,
          emotional unrest.

Take a deep breath.

That moment is a profound combination of hesitation, consideration, preparation, intention, action.

That *breath* envelopes us—body and spirit—and for a moment, we are suspended in this pivotal space. In that moment, there is clarity if we grasp it, there is courage if we embrace it, there is composure if we lean into it.

As you travel this contemplative journey, don't neglect these moments. *Often, take a deep breath.*

SURVIVAL—OUR COMMON RESPONSE TO SUFFERING

Suffering entered the story of our lives. We did not intentionally write it into the script. Yet, here it is. We recognize it. And it doesn't seem to have any thought of exiting the stage. Intentionally or unintentionally, survival kicks in.

One of our first attempts at survival is to *undo the change*. We desperately want to go back to that place where everything was—or where we thought it was—"all right." In the midst of our anxiety, we imagine that we must have been safe in that "before" place. We attempt to make the suffering disappear. The crisis is there in front of us, but we scramble to make it disappear, or at least make it blend into the landscape around us.

A common response is to put our suffering in a box, close it, and try to put life back together the way it was—or the way we thought it was.

It looks something like this:

What is it we are longing for?
The reality is that, from the moment of crisis, we are engaged in the search for *resolution*.

Resolution is the process of solving a problem. More specifically, resolution is the process of bringing problems to a *place of peace. To resolve something is to make peace with it.* This yearning for resolution seems to be a characteristic that was put into us by our Creator. Resolution is the way we survive, the way we endure.

Resolution is a good thing. It is right to come to a place of peace. But, two questions quickly follow:

How do we come to that place of peace?

Is it true peace or merely an act of quiet surrender and defeat?

37

Perhaps you have heard this advice: "Just put it aside and move on." It sounds like a good idea.

Here is our difficulty: We want to resolve the problem very quickly. We want to make everything okay. We want to put things back the way they were as soon as possible, so that we can continue our story, at least as we imagined it. Perhaps the urgency to bring resolution is for the sake of others. We want those around us to have the freedom to return to normalcy in their own lives. We don't want others to be concerned for us. There are many possible reasons for making a determined effort to resolve the issue of suffering and express an image of peace.

The result is that we often run swiftly to resolution before we really allow ourselves to feel the suffering. Rather than making peace with the suffering, even inviting it into the story, we quickly put it in a box and hide it away so that we—and others—cannot see it.

This might present a lovely visual to the audience but it turns our story inward in a way that prevents healing and destroys true peace. It leads us to an unhealthy place, a place that creates the perfect environment for infection.

Think about this scenario: As you are walking, you trip and fall, hitting your leg against a sharp rock. It cuts deep into your leg. Suppose you ignore it and continue with your day. You do not stop to care for it. After several days, the wound is infected and sore. You keep a bandage on it and wear clothing that keeps it from view, so that no one will see it and be offended.

The skin tries to grow back together, but underneath, there is infection. In fact, the poison in your leg begins to cause trouble in other parts of your body. Eventually, the wound will have to be opened and cleaned before your entire body can heal. There is no way to care for the extended pain without first giving full attention to *the original wound*.

And so it is with our suffering. If we superficially cover up our pain and hide it, we will never really be able to resolve, or come to peace with, the crisis that changed everything. We will also not be able to remove the poisonous infection that is now branching out from the original wound.

It is important for us to understand that suffering is normal and right following a crisis. This means allowing ourselves to feel the pain and hurt from the wounding event, even though the event might be over. For those who are bystanders, the empathetic pain lasts only through the first shocking moments. We hear about a hurricane, and we gasp at the destruction and the suffering. We shed tears; we listen to the news reports. Then, when the event is over, we go on with our lives. The victims, however, cannot walk away. They are trapped in the reality of their new story. There are many levels of suffering they have yet to experience.

But this time, it is not them. It is us. We find ourselves in our own suffering. Perhaps, at first, we are watching it as if from the outside, but we cannot walk away. This is now our story of suffering, with all its layers.

It is good and right that we allow ourselves to "feel" the pain.

The idea of engaging with suffering or investing in suffering might seem foreign to you, even inappropriate. Our natural instinct is to avoid suffering—at all costs!

What good could possibly come from embracing it? What benefit is there in walking towards suffering? What healing could come from lingering in that dark place that has caused such pain?

Our journey of healing will help us consider how we can suffer in a healthy way—in a way that is good for us.

On this journey, our first hurdle will be:

To look at suffering without attaching it to the primary focus of resolution.

In other words, as we begin this journey, we are not counting the days or the steps to completion and healing. The primary focus is to give attention to the pain, allowing ourselves to *feel*. In time, we will make peace with the suffering. But, it will not come as a quick fix. Resolution is not one determined jump; resolution is many small steps.

Notice the image of the path of resolution:

It is not a straight line. There are ups and downs.

RESOLUTION

An "up" might be that we make peace with some part of the pain, but the "down" is that other parts of the suffering are still powerful in our lives. At times, we might feel like we have reached some kind of resolution, and then suddenly we are confused and angry again. This is the natural and healthy trajectory of the journey. To use a wonderfully descriptive African phrase: resolution comes *slowly by slowly.*

So, simply let these truths settle in as an assurance to you:

Suffering entered your story.

> There is no need to hide it.

> There is no hurry to fix it.

> It is healthy and right to feel the pain.

This awareness will be beneficial as we take the next bend in the road.

Take a deep breath. It could be time to become familiar with suffering in a way that begins to bring peace.

14
BEGINNING TO FOCUS

Creating a timeline of your life at the previous bend in the road might have been a daunting task. You might have been surprised by the moments that were impressed into your memory. Remember, this journey is not about what "should" be or what someone else might think is important. This is your journey, and it is important to respond naturally and truthfully, acknowledging those moments that stir your heart.

To consider *all* the events in our lives would be ominous and overwhelming. So, as we move forward, we will begin to narrow our focus. Which moments will come up front and center? Which events will push their way forward, demanding attention? What emotions will surface, requiring that we seek out the source?

This is where the journey becomes very personal.

We are narrowing our line of sight, zooming in from the immense timeline of our lives to focus on those particular moments that have left their mark on us—those moments that shifted us to a place that is unfamiliar—a place where we have no explanations and no answers. Where we scramble for footing but cannot seem to find safe, solid ground.

Sometimes, such moments are profound and easy to identify. We can picture exactly when the moment happened and what destruction it caused. It is embedded in our memory, locked in place.

Other times, however, suffering enters our story more subtly. Perhaps, it began at a point in the past, and we didn't comprehend its destructiveness at the time. Or perhaps, it did not even begin as a negative or destructive experience, but along the way, the *safe* became *unsafe*. The *okay* took on adverse implications.

It is also possible to discover that our pain is wrapped up in a particular emotion or response that regularly plagues us. By focusing on this emotional struggle, we can eventually discover the source of that pain.

The awareness of suffering. It is much like a hidden disease that slowly poisons, little by little, until it becomes impossible to ignore that something is drastically wrong. Then, whether suddenly or gradually, the destructive circumstance becomes part of our story.

If you are considering this new journey, it is likely that you have experienced some kind of suffering. Perhaps, it was many years ago. Perhaps, it was recent. Perhaps, you are in the midst of it right now. Perhaps, you are in the discovery process. But something doesn't feel right. *What is it?*

On the previous bend in the road, you created a simple timeline, including a few events, positive and negative. Now, as we approach our next bend in the road, our focus will settle on a particular moment of suffering. You may have experienced more than one life-shaking or destructive event; however, it is best to bring one area of suffering into focus rather than to feel overwhelmed by all negative events at one time.

This part of the journey will be difficult, because in order to find the *one* moment, we must think of the *many.* So, as we start the next bend in the road, I will remind you to pause and—literally, physically—take a deep breath.

A BEND IN THE ROAD,
BEGINNING TO FOCUS

Your mind and your body are woven together so that one affects the other. Anxiety, stress, and fear are passed from body to mind and mind to body without your intention or awareness. Your mind is not thrilled with the assignment to intentionally think about suffering. The natural response is anxiety; perhaps, even panic. You can slow this process a bit by *helping your body help your mind.* This is a moment for you to be a good traveling companion for yourself.

Sit comfortably. Place your hands loosely in your lap. Intentionally breathe from your stomach, extending your stomach each time you inhale. Exhale with control. This is a *slow-down* moment. Count to three as you inhale and exhale. Ignore your mind (which is clamoring for attention) and concentrate on breathing deeply and slowly for several minutes. By giving your body the opportunity to calm down, you are encouraging your mind to move toward serenity as well.

Now, let's take some time at this bend in the road.

Think carefully about which experience or feeling of suffering needs your attention on *this* journey at *this* moment in time. Consider these possibilities:

- There may be several events of suffering that have the same source.

- There may be one event that is the source of immediate and then further suffering.

- There may be one emotion that overwhelms and paralyzes you. In this case, the emotion could be your focus; events or circumstances would come later.

This is not a quick decision. Take time to contemplate, to ponder. Set aside all distractions.

Eventually, one source of intrusion, one distress, one oppressive concern will rise to the surface. One area of pain will cry out for attention. When it does, write a few descriptive words below to identify it. There is no need to write the entire story. For now, simply identify *one connection* to your pain. This connection may change or broaden as time goes on. Right now, we are only beginning.

15

LIFE AS IT WAS, LIFE AS IT IS NOW

Let's ponder this for a bit. It is important to understand that life will never be exactly the same as it was before the crisis.

We may have pictured our lives—or some part of our lives— in a particular way. We knew it wasn't perfect but we envisioned potential and possibility for change.

All in all, we held onto the dream:

And then, circumstances changed, fears became reality, expectations fell apart.

We have come face-to-face with the reality:

We discovered that we are drawn toward resolution—that feeling of putting things back together again—and we express this by attempting to quickly put our lives back in order and move forward. But this can actually hinder healing and quell peace.

We need to think of *suffering and resolution as being connected* with a gentle, loosely held cord.

We do not give resolution permission to pull us forward with a voice that demands results and transformation.

We do not give suffering permission to hold us in a place of despair and defeat.

Resolution comes slowly by slowly.

So, we give ourselves grace for the journey.

And when we do come to peace,

it will not be with the way life used to be,
but *with the way life is now . . .*

with the scars, the wounds, the pain.

Life as it was? Perhaps, that life was only the way we imagined it—the way we hoped it would be.

And if we continue to try to *"re-create"* that life, we will find ourselves attempting to

undo the betrayals,

hide the effects of the abuse,

replace the loss,

cover the wounds,

rewrite the script of suffering.

We will remain in an unhealthy place.

In fact, that self-defensive action will actually cause us to suffer repeatedly, because as we struggle to recreate what life once was, our *new reality* will always—eventually and inevitably—come to the surface. And the crisis will repeat its initial hit. The moment of impact will be on continual replay.

Accusation, again. Disappointment, again. Betrayal, again.

There is a better way. We will know that we are beginning to travel down this better path, that we are beginning to heal in a healthy way, when we are able to make peace *with the way life is now.*

Maybe some of you have had the experience of walking hurriedly into a room, only to hit your foot on the leg of a chair or table, because it was not where you expected it to be. If we know the furniture in our home has been rearranged, it is wise to take a look in each room before we enter, so we know what to expect. Although this is a very simple illustration of what has happened in your life—it does not begin to touch the levels of pain, destruction, and *rearrangement* that have happened—it does help to describe an important part of this journey.

We will have many conversations along this journey of healing. Some will be more difficult than others. Some will lead to decisions. And some, like this one, will simply help us to discover truth or to become aware of and familiar with our pain. These types of discussions are important because the more we hide from the pain, the more threatening it becomes.

So, with that, let's be prepared for our next bend in the road. There, we will look at what life was (or what we thought it was) and what life now is.

A BEND IN THE ROAD
LIFE AS IT WAS,
LIFE AS IT IS NOW

It is time to open a door . . . or two. But let's do it gently. As we've learned, it can be harmful to go running through the house, throwing open doors, and rushing in. As a wise mentor said to me in my darkness, "Only push on the door that is already slightly open."

So, look for a door that is slightly ajar. You won't need to look far. In the previous bend in the road, you briefly described something that you could connect to your pain, whether that be an event or an emotion. That "something" you described is a slightly open door.

Jot down that description here, next to the image of the door.

Now... *push gently.*
Simply peer into the room on the other side.
What is arranged differently?
What has changed?

Look honestly. Do you remember how life looked before—or at least how you imagined it looked? Now, look just as honestly at the way it is—the way it became after your awareness of events or information. Write about the differences you see in the space below.

No words? Draw or sketch the changes you are feeling instead.

Avoid the why's, the what-if's, the reasons, all the details. Avoid jumping to conclusions about the next steps. Avoid everything else but *the honest expression of the "before" and "after" pictures of your life.*

16

BEAUTY IS

In the midst of suffering,

When the hues that color our lives are dark,

When the melodies play in a minor key,

When our words search only for another way to express the pain,

When our vision sees all through a shadowy veil of obscurity,

We forget that . . .

Beauty Is.

Quietly woven around you in your pain, Beauty Is.

The heavens declare the glory, and

the skies proclaim the work of the Creator's hands.

Day after day, they pour forth understanding;

night after night they reveal knowledge.

They have no speech, use no words;

No sound is heard from them.

Yet, their voices go out into all the earth;

their message to the ends of the world.

Beauty has not been destroyed.

You will discover it once again, perhaps in the most unlikely of places.

Beauty Is.

FAMILIARITY WITH SUFFERING

*Once suffering connects personally
with us, it is wise to respond in kind.
We have been properly introduced.
Now it is time to move
forward in the relationship.*

Many of us have read a book or watched a movie that began with one scene in the present and then took us to a flashback to explain how the characters arrived in their current circumstances. Once we know this backstory, we usually find ourselves responding to the current scene with more understanding and intensity. This is similar to where we find ourselves in our own stories.

The events of the past are very much a part of our current narrative. Some of us may be months, even years, down the road from the initial crisis. To help us understand ourselves now, we must comprehend how that initial suffering has shifted our perspective. That is, we must understand how it has changed the way we perceive all that happens around us.

At the first awareness of crisis, the pain can be so great, the fear so powerful, that we feel numb, even paralyzed. The onslaught of emotion consumes us. Nearly every piece of our lives connects and responds to the event in some way. We struggle just to survive.

Of course, we cannot continue in this crisis mode indefinitely, so a coping system sets in. We settle into a new normalcy. But often, we are not consciously aware that our perspective has changed immensely, that the suffering has affected so much about us, including how we think and reason— how we see "normal." In addition, although our immediate crisis response might have calmed down, our emotions and our bodies have not—they are still responding to that traumatic time.

We respond to life with a profound new perception . . .

- Our reasoning now includes the personal awareness of suffering and the existence of incomprehensible events.
- Our trust of others now includes the pain of betrayal.
- Our presumption of control now senses its limitations.
- Our planning and decision-making now include the very real possibility of danger and devastation.

Perhaps, we should have been aware of these realities previously; and in some subconscious or logical way, we probably were. Now, however, we are *experientially* aware.

This is a serious perspective shift. This new awareness burns its way deep into our being. Without requesting permission, it adds new hues, shapes, lights, and shadows to every image.

Most of us will not consciously adjust our perspective of life; rather, it will be adjusted for us, as our subconscious profoundly considers every detail of our overall experience—in particular, how our past experiences impact all current and future experiences.

Now, our subconscious filters our perception of life—including our choices, thoughts, impressions, emotions, relationships, and more—through . . .

the undeniable awareness of suffering
the inbuilt desire for resolution
and
the potential for repeated pain

These three unseen companions are with you, even if you are not conscious of them. Don't be afraid of them. Don't ignore them. Listen to the details they add to the conversations you have with yourself.

Sometimes, they work well together, and other times, they create confusion. One vies for attention and another pushes back. Sometimes they add positive discernment. Other times, they instill unjustified fear.

On this journey, you will discover how these new filters influence your choices, your relationships, and your sense of well-being. You will begin to recognize them in your conversations with yourself, in your responses to others, and in your decision-making.

But in order to see them, you must not be afraid to *look back*. Remember, a clear awareness of past events will give you the potential to respond with more understanding to the *current scene* in your narrative.

18

BECOMING FAMILIAR WITH SUFFERING

So far on this journey, we have talked about the idea of suffering and recognized that it has played a role in our life's story. We have also started to identify particular experiences of suffering in our life's story. Whether those experiences are . . .

> one-time events,

> a series of circumstances that finally come to a point of confrontation, or

> the realization or awareness of a previous event and its effects on us,

all of them, in some way, mark a period in time—a period that creates before-and-after pictures of our lives. In this book, I call such periods of impact, confrontation, and realization *crisis moments*. The *crisis moment* overwhelms us, whether suddenly or slowly, introducing suffering into our life.

Of all that we could wish to become "familiar with," suffering likely is not at the top of our list. Yet, once suffering connects with us personally, it is wise to respond in kind—because when we avoid it or deny its presence in our lives, its effects only grow stronger.

In other words, now that we have been properly introduced to suffering, it is time to move forward in the relationship. It is time to really *see* the suffering that has entered your story—to acknowledge its presence as something more than an event on a timeline; to recognize it as something real and personal. But take heart. For we will also discover along our journey that, although we will become familiar with our suffering, we will not be destroyed by it.

THE NEGATIVE EFFECTS OF SUFFERING

Before we can become more familiar with suffering and its lingering effects, we must talk about a word that we often see these days in conversations about suffering: *trauma*.

There are times when, even after the event, the negative effects of our suffering seize the opportunity to dig into our souls, settle down, and entangle themselves with every part of our life expression. The force of the suffering then intensifies and causes *trauma* in our lives.

Many of us might draw back from the implication that we have experienced trauma, because we think the word is reserved only for the world's worst-case scenarios. We might point to particular events of suffering that can be categorized as "traumatic," while believing that our crisis moment is not serious or dramatic enough to fit into that category. Or perhaps you just find it intimidating to add the "trauma" label to the already frightening reality of your suffering.

Whatever the case, *trauma* is simply a word that describes the negative after-effects of suffering—or the "after" picture of the crisis moment. The initial impact, confrontation, or realization stays with us, so that our wound grows deeper and begins to spread, reaching areas of our lives that were previously left untouched by the event.

As shown by the following "formula," trauma may begin with the event that caused the onset of suffering, but it also goes much deeper, resulting in moments of pain, confusion, and upheaval that can spiral and twist in and through our lives in the ensuing days, months, and even years:

TRAUMA = The Initial Crisis + All of the Pain, Confusion,
and Upheaval That Follow In Its Wake.

Trauma happens when the force of our suffering intensifies beyond the initial impact, not only touching—but overpowering—our former reactions and responses to life. It takes over the control center of our emotions, decision-making, and our responses in a way that makes us unable to function in a healthy and positive manner in the present. More particularly, it begins to affect our sleeping, our eating, our relationships with others, our work, and even our physical health.

Whether lurking about in the shadows or standing oppressively in full view, trauma is the *full impact of suffering* and poses a threat to all that is right and good and healthy in our lives.

Finally, it's important to point out that trauma is not the same thing as an emotional scar. A physical wound often leaves a scar—a place where an open wound has healed and no infection remains. A scar leaves visible evidence of the injury. When we look at the scar on our body, we remember the event that caused the injury. The scar might remain there forever, but it no longer has harmful control over our body.

In the same way, emotional suffering leaves emotional, spiritual, and sometimes even physical scars. These are places in our lives where healing has occurred and yet, left a mark. When we "look at" these types of scars, they, too, remind us of the initial crisis—and in that way, the crisis remains a part of our life forever. It is a permanent part of our story. But a scar does not cause us more harm.

Trauma, on the other hand, wants to prevent healing. Trauma continues to open the wound and then attempts to deepen and intensify it. Trauma wants to hold onto control. And it always wants more.

In that position of control, trauma takes on the temperament of a living thing. It has characteristics. It has patterns that we can observe and recognize. We feel its manipulation, its cruelty, its accusations. We suspect that it is undermining our intentions. It scatters around confusion and doubt. We wait for a reprieve, but it is persistent. Trauma leads us to believe that we have lost the ability to speak on our own behalf or to reason with good logic. Trauma whispers that we are undone.

The good news is that we can begin to take back control from trauma and move forward in healing—but we can only do that once we become familiar enough with the identity of trauma to recognize it and call it to accountability.

A BEND IN THE ROAD

BECOMING FAMILIAR WITH TRAUMA

We all know the red flags of a scam, whether it be by email or text or phone. Ahhh, we think. *This is a scam. This is an attempt to take me down a road that will be dangerous for me. I recognize this threat. I am familiar with this treachery, and I will not fall for it!* Because you are familiar with the characteristics and patterns of such deception, you can protect yourself and turn away.

In the same way, we can protect ourselves from trauma by becoming familiar with its characteristics and patterns. This understanding will help us to recognize the red flags in our lives. Familiarity with the negative effects of suffering will not make us weak; it will instill courage.

Let's do this together. Read about the characteristics of trauma below, and as you do, contemplate what they look like in your own life. Step back and consider them without self-defense. Focus on the raw reality of their presence in your life rather than on the "I shoulds." Record your thoughts in the margins using words, phrases, or exclamations—but most of all, using truth.

Characteristic #1: TRAUMA IMPAIRS OUR MEMORIES.

Stay with me. This is not to say that we are telling untruth, that we misunderstood, or that something didn't really happen. It happened! Yet, trauma insists on dumping all the memories into a large bucket and then challenging us to pull them out in perfect order and detail. In the process, sequence, names, dates, and exact words can easily become intertwined in a way that confuses us and others. Confusion is part of trauma's hold on us and often causes us to shut down, losing confidence and clarity.

There is more. Trauma causes us to forget, or set aside, most positive things. We forget our accomplishments. We forget our strengths. We forget our hopes. We forget anything good that happened during the time of suffering, even if it was unrelated to the particular event that caused our pain. We see the past and the future through the invisible veil of the pain, the fear, and other emotions created through that suffering.

Characteristic #2: TRAUMA CHANGES OUR VIEW OF OURSELVES.

A common response is to blame ourselves.

"I should have done . . . " and "Why didn't I do . . . ?" are commonly woven through our conversations, at least with ourselves.

We lose confidence and have difficulty making decisions.

Am I to blame? Am I imagining this? Could I have stopped it from happening? Am I crazy? I cannot trust myself again. Others are looking at me. I cannot cope with the simplest of tasks and decisions.

One moment, we think, *I don't need anyone.*

The next moment, *I do not want to be alone.*

In many ways, we don't seem to know ourselves anymore. We feel like we are outside looking in. We struggle to balance self-defense with self-accusation; self-pity with self-anger.

Characteristic #3: TRAUMA CHANGES OUR VIEW OF OTHERS

We might define others as foes, using illogical judgment to interpret a few words they said or a look they gave as being negative.

We might not be able to trust anyone, or we might trust people too easily!

We tend to think everyone else is just fine. *If I could only be in that position, we think.* Or, *No one has ever experienced what I am facing. They don't have time to listen to me. They'll think I am crazy or looking for attention.*

The truth is that trauma separates us from others.

We begin to draw into our own world
>   of pain,
>   of reasoning,
>   of self-conversation, and
>   of survival.

We even rewrite our stories in ways that become more acceptable or reasonable.

Characteristic #4: TRAUMA MANIPULATES OUR RESPONSES.

Every one of us responds to current situations based on our life experiences. Often, we are aware of this reaction as it is happening. Perhaps, we can even control our response if we are focused and aware.

However, trauma complicates things.

A sound, a building, a voice, or even a single word can take us, without warning, to that place of suffering. In an instant, we are there again. And our response flows from that previous experience rather than the current reality.

What prompts these unconscious responses? And why do we not see it coming?

The pain that we experience naturally connects to one or more of our senses —perhaps sound, smell, or touch. That sensory connection becomes a trigger. Triggers cause a response—usually an unconscious one. We do not stop to think logically and make a decision. The response is much more direct and immediate, often beyond our control.

Some triggers are obvious and expected; others catch us by surprise and we have no chance to put up a defense. Things that were harmless before, now betray us unexpectedly.

Trauma is clever in its manipulation, but it is illogical. It is based in the reality of the suffering and not in the current reality. However, our minds do not calculate this discrepancy. Instead, everything in us is swept away. The wound reopens. The pain and emotions flow through. And we are swept up and caught in that previous moment.

Characteristic #5: TRAUMA'S ATTACKS ARE ROOTED IN FEAR.

Trauma's manipulation does not take us to a confident and joyful place. The trigger, the reminder, the confusion—all take us to a place of fear and vulnerability. Without logic, we are terrified of the potential of that same suffering, that same pain: *What if it is happening again?*

Perhaps, we are fearful of feeling the shame, the pain, the impact of that previous event once again: *I barely survived before. I cannot feel that again.*

Fear can be debilitating, paralyzing. Fear can attack suddenly, or it can grow from a tiny seed that begins with the smallest of reminders. Fear is a powerful tool that trauma uses against us. Why? Because, it works almost every time to undermine and immobilize us.

These are the characteristics of trauma, which is *the full impact of suffering.*

Suffering *was* and suffering *is*. The pain, confusion, and upheaval initially settle in and eventually fade, blending into the surroundings. Yet, from its quiet hidden place, trauma continues to influence and infect. It is important for us to recognize its characteristics and its tactics. We must be able to discern when it is the trauma that is speaking so that we can firmly begin to disconnect.

Ah . . . do you see?

> *First*, become familiar. *Then* disconnect. In that order.

To disconnect first plants a seed of weakness and flight that tends to haunt us. We remain fearful of what could be around the next corner, what could surface that we want to keep hidden. Or we naively assume the pain is in the past, the wound is healed, and there are no scars.

To become familiar first plants a seed of strength. We are not cowering because of what trauma might do to us. We are opening our eyes to recognize the deception of its threat. This gives us the discernment and courage we need to disconnect from the negative influence it can hold over us.

Where does this leave us for this part of the journey?

We have been looking back to discover that the initial suffering has lingered with us and taken up residence. We know that we will encounter it in various ways—some expected, some unexpected— and that many of our responses will be influenced by it.

We also gathered truths that will help us to move forward on our journey; in particular, we created a "profile" of trauma. Tuck it away as useful information. We will refer back to this conversation at various bends in the road.

Finally, rest assured that you will find protection as you become familiar with trauma's tactics. Perhaps from this conversation, you are beginning to recognize them already.

19

HOW DO YOU FEEL?

People often ask, "How are you feeling?"

At times I want to respond, "I wish you could look inside my mind, my heart, my very soul . . . then you could *see* how I feel."

But, we are limited to responses like, "Sad, Hurt, or Angry." These words do not do justice to the intensity, detail, and depth of what we feel, including what we sense physically, mentally, and spiritually. The inadequacy *of words* keeps us from telling our stories.

Pictures, though, can give voice to feelings. Pictures can provide an expression of emotions that cannot be described with words.

Therefore, this part of the journey provides images to help you begin the story. It nudges on the door labeled, "How do you feel?"

We have come to a bend in the road.

A BEND IN THE ROAD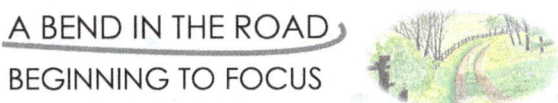
BEGINNING TO FOCUS

How do you feel?

>How do you feel now?

>How did you feel at the time of the crisis?

>What feeling drives your everyday responses?

>What feeling do you find most difficult to express in words?

The images[1] provided on the following pages can help you express the unspoken emotions that arise in response to these questions. They can be your voice.

As you peruse each one, you might simply point to a picture and say, "*This. This is how I feel . . . or how I felt.*" Or a picture might throw open the door to words and phrases and expressions that tumble out, one on top of the other, grateful to finally be heard. Either way, the narrative begins.

Consider the following as you move around this bend in the road:

- Allow yourself to respond truthfully from that raw place deep within. Your responses might surprise you. Remember to be compassionate with yourself and encourage honesty.
- Avoid correcting or reprimanding yourself. This is a time of expression, not right or wrong.
- The images portray men, women, old and young, and various cultures. Don't let the identities of those portrayed guide your responses. Connect with the action, the perspective, the feeling that each image opens in you.
- There is no need to respond to all the images. Particular ones will speak to you.
- Do not feel the need to explain why the image speaks to you as it does. This experience is to open a path of connection. If it leads to words, good. If not, good. The connection from suffering to expression has been traveled, and that is the forward movement you want.
- Use the extra space provided around the pictures to add phrases, words, or your own pictures—whatever helps you narrate the "how you feel" of your suffering.
- Give yourself the freedom of time and space.
- Know that any feeling evoked might not be your entire expression of suffering. It might speak only to one small moment in your narrative. That's okay.

Take your time. You are not racing toward a finish line. You are experiencing the journey. This might be a part of the journey to which you return often.

Listen, be a good companion, provide a safe place—so that your story can be heard.

---

[1] All images were purchased from Dreamstime with a royalty free license.

65

20

MY TRAVELING COMPANION

I have implied that there is another person on this journey with us. I have referred to Him as our traveling companion. I don't want that to feel strange to you. I also don't want it to be confusing or evasive. So, let's talk about it.

I must include Him because He is such a vital part of my story, both of suffering and of healing. You will learn more about this as we move forward. I also understand that you might not yet see or acknowledge Him as part of your story. That is okay.

Who is He? His most common name is God. And yet, even that name brings multiple thoughts and even images to mind. Each of you has your own concept of who God is and what part He plays in our lives. Perhaps, this is the reason I have been a bit vague about His role. I am concerned about the assumptions, and even, the suspicions, that might come to mind as I speak of His interactions with us. My hope is that you will become familiar with Him in a safe and genuine way. At the same time, there is no pressure to embrace a particular way of thinking or to follow a particular spiritual journey.

There is simply an introduction to this eternal One, who knows you, who sees you, who loves you, and who values you beyond any other one you have encountered.

You will meet Him in my story with a variety of names:

Creator: He created all things, including each of us. In fact, you have eternal and unchangeable value because you are His perfect creation.

LORD: He is ruler of all—the perfect presence of justice and authority. There is no one else who can adequately fill this position of protection for us.

I AM: The One who exists from eternity past to eternity future; the One who can answer all my doubts and accusations with "I AM."

Father: As our father, God is our guide and protector. This term of *father* may not bring comfort to some. However, God is all that we ever wanted or expected from a father. He is safe. He is loving. He is kind. He is a protector.

Jesus: This "God-as-man" is the embodiment of God, also called "God with us." He lived on this earth and still connects with us in our humanness. He is our fellow sufferer.

The Good Shepherd: He protects, guides, rescues, and cares for us on this treacherous and sometimes, frightening, journey.

Savior: He is the only one who can rescue, reclaim, and save us.

Whenever you see this companion enter my story, I encourage you to keep an open mind. I do not want you to be puzzled or troubled when you see Him woven in and through the narrative. I assure you that He is safe and compassionate. He knows your unspoken story. He sees you as you desire to be seen. He loves you with purity. He values you as a priceless gem.

I have found Him to be my perfect and trusted traveling companion.

21
I AM NOT CONSUMED

"If I look at my suffering, if I face my trauma . . . it will destroy me; it will consume me." Perhaps, you have said something similar, or at least sensed this possibility deep inside.

Long ago, there was a man who may have had the same fear. Then he took the bend in the road and discovered truth that helps us on our own journeys:

> I remember my affliction and my wandering,
>
> the bitterness and the gall.
>
> I well remember them,
>
> and my soul is downcast within me.
>
> Yet this I call to mind
>
> and therefore I have hope:
>
> Because of the LORD's great love we are not consumed,
>
> for His compassions never fail.
>
> They are new every morning;
>
> great is Your faithfulness."
>
> (Lamentations 3:19–23)

This man looked at his suffering clearly. He recalled the details. ("I remember my suffering.") He saw God's goodness during his suffering ("the LORD's great love"). He saw that there were boundaries to the effects of his suffering ("I am not consumed.") And then, he spoke of love. ("His compassions never fail.")

For many of us, the idea of love has been tainted with bitterness and betrayal. Whether love from a parent, a spouse, a child, a grandparent, a sibling, a friend, the expectation of what love is, how love would be expressed to us—that expectation was broken, maybe even shattered.

The resulting pain crushed our very souls. That loss of right and good love threatened to completely consume and destroy us.

But hear the assuring words "Because of the LORD's great love . . . we are not consumed."

Perhaps, like me, you find it difficult to trust or even accept love. But I want to tell you what I have discovered:

> There is One who loves you with a great love.
> A loyal love. A faithful love. A pure love.

It is because of *that great love* for me that I have not been destroyed.

It is because of *that great love* for you that you have not been destroyed.

What a precious and profound truth to carry with us on this journey:

> *I remember my suffering.*
>
> *I am not consumed.*

We have covered some important ground on our journey so far.

- We briefly visited some events and emotions that have made up our story, both before and after suffering arrived on the scene.
- We spent time becoming familiar with the idea and character of suffering and even with the idea of prolonged pain, confusion, and upheaval—the trauma—that follows in its path.
- We also began to connect personally to this idea of suffering, recognizing its role in our current lives by simply allowing ourselves to see it and to give attention to it. *Yes, there it is. I acknowledge that suffering is part of my story.*

Now, it is time to move closer. It is time to connect with not just the *idea* of suffering in our life but also with the actual events and emotions of that suffering.

The event. The emotions. The ensuing period of suffering. How do we express it? Perhaps, like me, there came a time on this journey when you found just a few concise words to express the suffering.

How strange it felt. Words cast into the atmosphere, hanging there with heaviness. So profoundly full—and empty—at the same time. Nothing more to be said . . . and yet, so much more to be said.

This strange feeling occurs because we are connected to our suffering by more than just human-defined words. To know our suffering more intimately, we must look at it and express it in different ways—in ways connected to other senses, the way we did on our previous bend in the road, when we connected our emotions to pictures. But what about creating your own picture? Instead of connecting to an image that someone else has created, what would it look like if you put your emotions into your own visual image?

Maybe you have had your suffering in a box for a long time. Our next bend in the road might help you to lift the lid gently and begin a conversation.

A BEND IN THE ROAD
A PICTURE

Today we are going to allow our hands to express some of what we see and feel within, using them to create visuals on the page. These visuals might be . . .

> simple pictures,
>
> words,
>
> colors,
>
> or markings on the page that say, "I am here. I feel pain."

This expression of the suffering is for no one else. This opportunity for a contemplative moment is for you. This expression of pain, of suffering is *by* you and *for* you. Only *you* need to understand.

This is just one of the ways we will use to embrace our suffering. One of the ways we can become more familiar with it and claim it as our own. One of the ways we express it openly without fear.

Use colored pencils, crayons, markers, or whatever you want to add pieces of your suffering to this page. No rules. No requirements. No need for others to interpret. You might sketch an image of something that relates to your pain. Or you might use only colors and shapes to express your emotion.

Meditate. Ponder. Listen. Feel.

Then, allow your hands to draw your emotions as you express some portion of your story.

My eyes get weary. My mind gets weary. My emotions get weary. Periodically, while writing, I must *look away*.

My eyes need a rest from the strain of the computer screen.

My mind needs a rest from searching for the best way to communicate through words on the page.

My emotions need a rest from the intensity of the subject.

I imagine that you also need a moment to look away.

At initial points of suffering, we are compelled to give it our full attention. As time goes on, trauma picks up on this tendency to focus on the suffering. It attempts to convince us that we must remain under the control of that pain . . .

constantly,

relentlessly,

consumed.

It is at this place—after the initial intensity of the event—where we begin to remove trauma's control. It is at this point that we now may choose when and how much of the pain to engage with at any point in time.

We have the privilege to grasp one portion of the suffering and consider it, with the understanding that we can return it to its proper resting place.

We have times when we look at it with focus and intensity. We face suffering and fear. We clarify truth.

And then we need a rest . . .

> from the strain of the images.

> from the searching for words and expressions of our story,

> from the intensity of the the bends in the road.

We need to *look away*.

Remember, you are on a journey—not in a race. You have time and the control to look away as needed. Take walks. Enjoy a project. Set this journal aside for some days, if need be.

> Your eyes will rest.

> Your mind will clear.

> Your emotions will settle.

You do not need to be afraid to look at your suffering. You also have freedom to *look away* for a time.

SPEAKING TRUTH INTO SUFFERING

*Our Creator gives us value
that protects us and releases us
from the initial all-consuming control
with which the pain first grasped us.*

24
TO BE FULLY KNOWN

On my first stay at a refugee camp, while working in Thailand, I did not think to take a mirror. So, I peered into the tiny square of my eye-shadow compact. After two weeks, we made a trip to the city of MaeSot. At one location, I went into the ladies room, only to be confronted by a large mirrored wall. I actually jumped and audibly exclaimed! There I was—and not looking exactly as I had imagined!

My perception of how I looked had been based on how I felt inside. I was full of joy in the work I was doing, I was invested in delightful relationships, I was physically well, and I had a deep awareness of being where I was to be, doing what I was to be doing. My life was looking good. And in my mind, this translated to looking good physically, as well. But, that was not the case. The heat and humidity had taken over my hair and skin. All in all, I was a little disheveled.

I have also experienced the reverse. A new dress, a little makeup, a good hair day—and to everyone around me, all looked well in my life. But underneath, there was darkness, confusion, and panic.

We are such complicated creations. If you could actually look into a mirror and see YOU—mind and body, heart and soul—the image would astound you. There would be layer upon layer and multiple dimensions. There would be emotions weaving about, sometimes quiet and sometimes exploding. There would be thought patterns that seem confusing, yet when followed, begin to make sense and feel familiar. There would be wide pathways that you recognize and narrow trails leading to hidden caves that feel foreign and ominous. And so much more! Compared with the appearance that you were used to seeing, such a vivid, multidimensional image might startle you. It might feel as though, up until this point, you had been looking at yourself in a minuscule mirror and not seeing much at all!

Our culture attempts to condense and simplify the expression of our identity to a few visible characteristics. That generic-image template assigned to us is then used to instill guilt, dissatisfaction, greed, and shame. Those are the well-worn pathways we see when we look in the mirror. We tend to travel them often, running past the little trails that so badly need our attention.

Along our journey, though, we inevitably discover a few of those narrow trails and hidden caves. When you do, I encourage you not to avoid them. Don't be afraid to visit and see the multiple dimensions of YOU. Much of how we describe ourselves—much of the "I" and "me" we express—is based on what others expect from us. But there is so much more. And it is unique, remarkable, fascinating, and valuable.

In fact, your Creator would not be surprised at all to see this vivid, complete, multidimensional image of you. It is the YOU He always sees. He tells you Himself that you are "fearfully and wonderfully made" (Psalm 139:14). He even uses the very image of a mirror to show us this: "For now we see only a reflection as in a mirror…[we] know in part," but one day, we will "know fully even as [we are] *fully known*" (1 Corinthians 13:12 emphasis mine).

Imagine that! *We* only know *ourselves* in part. Others know us only in part too. Yet we long to be *fully known.* And who but our Creator could know us in that way? He knows us gently and compassionately. That is why He is such a good and trustworthy companion on this journey. He sees us. He knows us. And He loves us.

Have you said those words? Maybe you have thought them, but did not speak them aloud. Or maybe, it wasn't even a conscious thought but simply a resignation within your spirit:

This is just my life.

As I think back over the years, I now understand that those five words had settled into my being, deeper and deeper, year after year. That mindset and heart-set colored my actions and responses. It showed that I had resigned to the presence of doubt and pain in my life.

We are to *come to peace* with the way life is now—not *resign* to it. How are these two things different?

Let's talk about it.

It is natural to be uncomfortable and maybe a bit weary of those who are constantly complaining and wishing for a different set of circumstances. We don't want to be one of those people. After all, *contentment is a spiritual virtue.*

But we step into a destructive place when we submit, without reason, to "this is just my life." We step into a dangerous spot when we set aside all consideration of what is right and good for us.

I have said it in a variety of relationships: "I don't think this is what love is supposed to feel like. This friendship is causing anxiety. I feel like I have no value. I feel used. I am weary of it all. Oh well. *This is just my life.*"

It is shocking how often I have acquiesced to the script I imagined was "right." As if I was standing in the shelter of a tree, only to find that the branches were obscuring my vision to the truth I needed so badly. It would have been wise for me to move aside the branches that kept me from seeing clearly how I should proceed. Perhaps, you have had the same experience.

At times, it is necessary to balance two truths at the same time:

We can have *patience and mercy with others,*

>*keep the peace,*

>AND *protect our bodies and spirits in a healthy way.*

We can have both *contentment*

>AND *a correct awareness of truth and justice.*

How do we correctly and peacefully allow such seemingly contradictory concepts into our journey? There are no definitive formulas or step-by-step directions for this balancing act, because every story is different. Every narrative is unique. However, there are principles—thoughts and attitudes —that can guide us in the right direction. These principles create a protective covering over us, providing us with a new shade tree made up of branches of truth—branches that provide protection rather than deception. When circumstances rain down upon us, they first come up against these principles of truth that protect us:

>I am a unique and intentional creation by the Perfect Creator.

>I am fully known and declared valuable by the Perfect Creator.

>I am loved.

>I am fearfully and wonderfully made.

>I am fully known.

How can the branches of this shade tree protect us?

The value given to us by our Creator covers our bodies, our spirits, our very souls from all that rains down on us.

When it does rain, understanding our worth does not mean making a self-centered "I don't deserve this!" cry toward the heavens. Rather, it is a profound awareness that the value given to me by my Creator sets a boundary to those abusive actions and impressions and words that shout at me that I am not worthy of protection.

And it is out of this awareness of my value as a unique creation that I discern and acknowledge threats to my body and to my spirit.

Without this protective awareness, there is the great potential that abuse, manipulation, lies, unwise choices, and confusion will harm us. How often have we stood with these destructive forces raining down upon us, as we cower, longing for someone to see us as valuable? How often have we submitted to the lies and accusations?

Having an awareness of the value given to us by our Creator allows us to interact with others from a perspective of clarity—a healthy perspective. We no longer need to endure or respond to abuse simply to find identity, feel value, or gain approval. Instead we can acknowledge that

I already have extravagant value,
unable to be blemished or depreciated by others.

This guiding principle of our worth gives us the courage needed to balance truths that seemingly contradict each other. Our unchangeable value that is held and protected by God gives us the foundation to embrace both *contentment* and *a correct awareness of truth and justice.*

So, what goes wrong in the conversation as it plays out in our minds? The opposite of being content, of course, is being discontent. Sometimes discontent stems from selfishness or from the desire to create a false impression of our identity. This type of discontent is something we want to avoid; it leads only to bitterness. But other times, discontent stems from a unsettled spirit or is a response to abuse or the presence of evil. It is good to acknowledge this type of discontent. When we don't, when we instead try to bury or run away from it or push it aside, we resign to the heart attitude that "this is just my life." But this is not truly an attitude of contentment and will not lead to peace. Deep down, the unsettledness remains, because we know that we sidestepped truth and allowed evil to continue. As difficult as it may be, when we instead acknowledge our discontent with evil, we enable truth and justice, and that makes us truly content in the long run.

And, what do we do with the desire to *show patience and mercy to others, keep the peace, and also protect our bodies and spirits in a healthy way?*

Keeping the peace is good. It is right to be a peacemaker, rather than one who stirs up discord. However, there are times when truth and justice cause unsettledness. So, in order to live truthfully and rightly,

at times we must be conduits of *mercy*, and
at times we must be conduits of *justice*.

In other words, we seek peace, but not at the cost of harm to the oppressed and abused. In fact, our Creator's heart is also for the weak and the oppressed (which is why He is such a good protector of your story);

"Defend the weak and the fatherless; uphold the cause of the poor and the oppressed." (Psalm 82:3)

"Learn to do right; seek justice." (Isaiah 1:17)

Show mercy? you might wonder. Yes, but protection of abuse is *not* a valid expression of mercy. We also do not give mercy out of fear or in response to manipulation by another. We do not give mercy to the detriment of the weak. We speak up for the abused, and in so doing, we may be used as a conduit of justice.

These ideas and truths—

that we can heed our unsettled spirit,

that we can be used for mercy *and* justice,

that we can balance the desire to be a peacemaker with an unwavering heart to protect the oppressed—

provide a gentle, yet sometimes powerful, guide in *the fragile balancing act of peace, contentment and unsettledness.* Conversely,

"This is just my life" expresses *painful resignation.*

"This is just my life" suppresses our story in an unhealthy way.

"This is just my life" leads to unwise choices and paves the pathway for further abuse.

So, what do we do with this phrase? We leave it at the side of the road. Are there ways of coming to peace with suffering? Yes. Are there ways of living with pain? Yes. But, not one of them include, "This is just my life."

Let's move on to the next bend in the road.

Take some time to think carefully about the questions that follow.

Write down your thoughts and add any of your own questions.

Walk down a few of the narrow trails, bringing to light the YOU that longs to be fully known. The One who knows you fully is close beside you.

Does your view of *self* include taking on the responsibility for inflicted pain or abuse? Do you see yourself as "deserving" this pain or abuse in some way?

Does your view of others include justification for their abusive behavior?

Are you beginning to *accept* additional suffering and abuse, or even *expect* it?

Is your general life perspective growing more dim?

Do you respond to pain by becoming more withdrawn—from interactions with others, from relationships, or from engagement in daily activities?

Do you insist on "good" behavior from yourself towards others even when abuse and mistreatment are clearly evident?

Are you learning to embrace your worth, capability, and strength?

Your path is unique.
Take time to ponder the blessings
and the challenges . . .
the joy and the suffering . . .
the bright hues and the dark shades.
Avoid not one bend in the road.
All weave the exquisite tapestry of your life
with perfect design.

27
A BEGINNING AND AN END

We are becoming ever more familiar with the suffering that has touched our lives. We have opened our eyes to its traumatic effects that want to consume. We know that trauma, if left to its own devices, will envelop every part of our being—body, mind, and soul. Yet, we have been open to giving suffering its day. We have looked; we have felt; we have engaged.

We have also been given the opportunity to step away from that initial all-consuming control with which pain first grasped us. We can stand outside the swirling hurricane of confusion that first enveloped our lives. We can take one part of the suffering and look at it for a time—and we alone determine how much and for how long. The suffering and trauma need no longer be in control.

The next step in our journey will be to speak truth into the reality of our suffering. Our next bend in the road will help us do just that.

A BEND IN THE ROAD,
A BEGINNING AND AN END

I will caution you now—this is one of the more difficult bends in the road—but I will also encourage you: as you move past this bend, you will have discovered a valuable tool that you will use often.

At this bend in the road, it is time to take a closer look at your suffering. We will not so much look at the emotion of the suffering but rather the timetable of the suffering. As you can imagine, this will require that you intentionally and clearly think about the *details* of the event.

This will feel contradictory to your instinct to run away from the details, far and fast, but such an examination is necessary if you are going to honestly contemplate the source of your suffering. So, take heart: *you can do this*. And you will be stronger and freer because of it.

Together, we will take it slowly, step by step.

STEP 1

The first step is to think of the *very first thing* that happened in your crisis —what began your time of suffering. Consider this carefully. It may be difficult. It might not be obvious. And you might need some careful and quiet contemplative time to identify this honestly.

This is a good time to look back at the picture you drew. That picture was a visual expression of part of your story—part of your suffering. It is also a good time to look back at the original timeline you drew of your crisis event. Note however, that the timeline of your crisis event *is not the timeline of your suffering*. Suffering bleeds over the lines, into both past and future. We cannot put a start line or stop line on suffering; however, we can, over time, learn to rein in its grasp of control on us.

As you ponder this, you may initially feel that you have always been in pain. But, if we are talking about an event in your life, there was an initial moment of inflicted pain—or of the awareness of pain.

Or perhaps, as it was for me, there were multiple points of pain awareness—there was the initial impact, and then new realizations and new information came, time and again, increasing the intensity of my awareness. There was pain, then new pain, then more pain. Newly revealed truths opened my eyes to suffering that had begun long before the initial impact of awareness.

This journey of suffering is often not direct and easily plotted. So, trust yourself. Ask the questions. And then listen to yourself with full attention.

When was the first moment you felt unsafe?

When was the first time you felt threatened?

What was your first clue that all was not as it should be?

Draw a timeline on the last page of this chapter. With just a few words, describe that moment or experience at the beginning of that timeline. When you are done, return to this page and continue onto the next step.

STEP 2

Your second step might be even more difficult than the first. We want to discover the point in time when the actual threatening event ended.

Now, this is tricky. Remember that one of trauma's characteristics is to keep us in a state of fear and panic. The feelings of danger, threat, and vulnerability linger even after the immediate danger is over. Illogical fear encroaches into everyday life, settling in for the long haul. We must push past our feelings and discern the reality.

Think about the sequence of events in your crisis as follows: *beginning, end,* and *response.*

In most crises, there is a time when the actual event is over and the *response* to that event begins. For example, think with me about my mother's death. In November 2000, I received the call telling me that my mother had ovarian cancer. That was the moment of impact—the beginning—for that crisis in my life. On September 8, 2001, early in the morning, this crisis ended with my mother's physical death. Her journey of suffering was over. She passed from this life to the next. From that point on, any suffering or trauma I experienced was a *response* to the crisis. There was no longer a threat to her life. There was no longer suffering for her. The suffering would continue for me, but the event had ended. When I think of the event that I call "My Mother's Death," I think of things that happened from the beginning through the end of the event and then things that happened during the response time. However, the *threat* of the event is now over.

Some events seem to continue for a long time—unfolding, changing, perhaps growing in intensity. I experienced one event in which, over time, I continued to gain more and more awareness of evil and betrayal. Each time I thought the crisis had peaked, it rose to a new level. Only now can I look back and discern the moment when the actual *threat* of the event came to an end and the response began. Sometimes, I still question whether it is over. As I consider this event carefully, I understand that most of the remaining effects are now responses to the actual event. Have some of those responses turned into actual crisis events? Yes. But, those merit their own individual timelines. And each one has its own beginning and an end.

So, think very carefully. At what moment did the immediate threat diminish?

Or at what moment did the action of the crisis event end?

This might be when the actual physical threat to you came to an end.

Or it might be when some final bad news was given to you.

Perhaps, you need more than one descriptive moment in time for this. Go back to your timeline and, in just a few words, describe that moment or experience at the end of the line.

What if the suffering is still ongoing? Then it is helpful to discover smaller beginnings and endings within the event. Perhaps there was a difficult encounter that was necessary, a particular physical challenge, or even an especially distressing day of "life as it is now." Make small timelines for these and note the beginning and the end of each.

That confrontation that you had to face? It had a beginning and it had an end. You need not carry it forward with you and remain under its threat or control. Recognizing these moments of experience and closure are important. It protects you, so that months and years of suffering do not hang over you and hold you in place waiting for some definitive moment of relief.

When you have completed this step, return to this page and continue.

STEP 3

Good work. Take a deep breath. Now, look carefully at your timeline: There was a time when the crisis event began. And there was a time when the crisis event ended.

There was a beginning and there was an end.

Such a short sentence. Such a necessary truth.

It is dangerous and stressful to live as if we are still in the middle of an event when, in fact, it has ended. There can be no forward movement on the journey of healing until we understand the following:

The necessary *response* to the suffering still exists.

The consequences of the suffering may still be falling into place.

The emotional fall-out from the event is not over.

But . . .

the actual event itself has happened,

the immediate danger is over, and

very likely, there was a beginning and an end.

When we discover and accept this truth, we begin to put boundaries on the traumatic effects of the suffering. This is a dramatic and pivotal bend in the road. You will use this truth whenever the suffering threatens to overwhelm you in the same way it has in the past.

Yes, the traumatic event has a place on the timeline of your narrative. You will give it that space. But you will not allow it to take over the entire narrative. It had its beginning, and it had its end.

Go to your timeline. Put your finger on the part that marks the event's end. Circle it. You might need to return to this reminder again.

RESPONDING TO LOSS

We might recognize it immediately
or it may take some time,
but the root of our suffering
is that something is lost.
And that loss demands our attention.

As we are becoming familiar with suffering and its effects, which like to settle in, claim control, and entangle themselves in our lives as if they want to become our very identity, we must recognize that the expression of this turmoil is unique to each person.

Even if you and I have experienced a similar crisis, the characteristics of your suffering as it plays out in your life are different from mine. The "look" of your suffering is different from mine, even when there are similar circumstances.

We can read books about suffering—the way it looks, feels, and is defined. We can read another person's story of suffering and recognize some of the details or reactions. And yet, there are bits and pieces and twinges of feeling that are not the same. There are nuances that we can't identify with. We always walk away saying, "That's almost it . . . but not quite." This is not because we are not thinking or responding correctly; it is because our stories are all unique. If we are to move through healing, we must become familiar with our own individual narrative.

I wish we could sit together and talk about your journey so far. Is it difficult? Is it intriguing? Does it move you toward strength? Or, is it overwhelming? I have thought of you as I write this and considered how you might be feeling at this point in the journey. Perhaps you have spent years avoiding your suffering, assuming that healing would come if you pushed forward with good intentions. Now, you are courageously raising your head to see, tell, and hear your story. Whatever the case, your story is valuable in the specific way that you experience and express it.

But while the details of every story are different—the suffering is personal, and the trauma that follows is unique—there are common seeds that trauma sows in each of us.

Think of it this way: When the crisis occurs, seeds of suffering are sprinkled into our lives. Roots quickly grasp for a stronghold under the surface. Then follows the evidence of suffering as revealed through unique foliage. No two plants are the same. The tiniest nuances in outgrowth express each individual's personal expression of pain. However, there is a particular root of suffering that we all have in common. Do you see it? There is a *taproot* that feeds all other branching roots as well as the above-ground expression of the pain.

We might recognize it immediately, or it may take some time—but, in every trauma, in every suffering, there is the taproot of *loss*.

It is difficult to define *loss*. In its most basic form, it is the absence of something or someone. But it is possible to *feel* that absence. There is a common expression I learned when I lived in Nigeria: "I went to your house to see you, but all I met was *your absence*." The absence itself is *something*.

Especially in suffering, absence is not *nothing*. Absence is *something*. It is tangible to our spirits, our souls, and even our bodies.

If something is gone, why go looking for it? Why are we leaning in, actually looking for loss, especially when doing so is painful? Why not hide it or, better yet, snip that root of suffering—that loss—so it cannot cause more grief?

Think about the the death of a loved one. Can you imagine if we never mentioned that person's name again? If we refused to talk about her, quickly replaced her, and put away anything that reminds us of her? That would be so sad and very unhealthy.

Loss *IS*. Loss demands attention in some way. If we are to move toward healing, we must identify it and give it the attention it desperately longs for.

Doing so is not an accusation of or attack on your well-being. Rather, it is a loving conversation with yourself to say, "What are you missing? What was taken from you without your permission? Let's acknowledge what is gone." It is a gift of love and nurturing to yourself to acknowledge and talk about something that is causing pain.

So, where do we begin?

The next two bends in the road include several layers. We will not embrace them all at once but will take small, intentional, steps in a particular order:

- Acknowledge the loss. Identify the loss.
- Respond to the loss without attempting to replace it.
- Mourn the loss.

Please do not jump ahead. Be a patient and compassionate traveling companion for yourself.

In the upcoming bend, we will begin with the need to acknowledge and identify loss.

ACKNOWLEDGE AND IDENTIFY THE LOSS

It is fairly obvious to us that things have changed since the crisis. But often, we do not stop to think carefully about *what we have lost*. Because of the *crisis*, something is gone. It is not simply that all the elements of our lives have been moved about; this incorrect view leads us to the misconception that if we just find the pieces and put them all back together the way they were, there will be peace. Rather, there are elements that are now *missing*. If it were possible even to attempt the task of putting all the pieces back together as they were, we would eventually find that some of the pieces were gone. Those pieces—whether they went missing after the crisis or were never actually there in the first place—are *our loss*.

Some loss is obvious. It is easy to see *loss* when a fire takes a house, when war or disease takes a life, or when a thief takes possessions. These losses are visible and we recognize them clearly.

Such obvious, visible losses, however—although very important—can take over and conceal less evident layers of loss. After a housefire, for example, one might be so consumed with finding a new place to live or with repairing damages, that once the immediate needs are met, the person (along with those helping) assume the problem is resolved. Then it's back to life as normal. But there are further elements of loss that need attention.

Many layers of loss are often vague and hidden. Under the surface, there is inexplicable turmoil because the true extent of the loss has not been identified. To identify those additional layers, to identify the true extent of the loss, takes time, honesty, and effort. But this is a valuable part of the journey. This is a part of cleansing the wound.

There are other times when there is *no visual expression of loss*. We cannot point to an item or a person and say, "That was here, and now it is gone."

But hidden, intangible loss in any form is powerfully intrusive, destructive, and consuming.

- A person who is abused loses a sense of protection, trust, and value.
- A man who must flee for his life as a refugee loses his sense of strength and honor as he also loses his ability to defend his family.
- Alcoholism leaves a path scattered with the loss of identity, value, courage, and security.
- The breach of a precious relationship sweeps away one's sense of safety and trust.
- The loss of a child includes the loss of hopes and dreams for grandchildren and momentous occasions.

The list of invisible losses that we can experience is long and painful. We will have some of these losses in common with others and many that are unique to us.

RESPOND TO THE LOSS WITHOUT TRYING TO REPLACE IT

Loss is a strong common root of trauma. Much of our suffering after trauma is our response—the sadness, anger, and fear that we feel—to *what has been lost*. Our trust was broken; our love was forsaken; our feeling of safety was destroyed. In response to our current losses, we feel that future events are no longer possible or that the years we gave to someone in trust are now wasted and worthless. Instincts take over in our defense.

Our defensive responses to loss often play out in one of two ways:

1. We minimize or downplay the loss, saying things like,

    > "It isn't that bad,"

    > "I don't need that,"

    > "I will be fine. I will just rebuild,"

    > or

    > "Others have it worse than I do."

    A woman may say to her friend who has lost a child, "Be grateful that you still have two other children." Someone may say to a girl who was abused, "I know someone who had a much worse experience than you did. Be grateful your experience was really not so bad."

    These assurances do not calm the ache; they only make us feel guilty. They silence our expression of pain. But, deep inside we *feel the absence.* Something or someone has been *taken away against our wishes,* and no attempt at a reassuring comparison will make it vanish.

2. We attempt to replace whatever we lost as soon as possible.

    A mother who lost a child might want to have another child immediately. After the loss of a relationship, someone may quickly try to fill the void. We quickly rebuild the house or cover the scars.

But when we try to replace what we lost too quickly, we only cover up the pain. We also make poor decisions when we focus on filling the emptiness. Thus, the choices that come from this instinctive reaction to protect ourselves actually lead to more suffering.

Loss. Something important is gone. There is an empty place where once there was . . .

some person,

some expectation,

some unspoken longing,

some trust,

some possibility,

some promise of joy . . .

Now, our spirits feel the *absence*. Our bodies feel the *absence*.

And this is the bend in the road to which we come.

A BEND IN THE ROAD
DISCOVERING LOSS

At this bend in the road, we will open ourselves up to an honest and painful awareness of loss.

This is part of hearing our own story. This is part of being a good companion on the journey. We dare not make light of it, saying it doesn't matter. We must not feel guilty for the sadness that loss brings to us. It is important that we *see* the loss.

Maybe you know that a bad thing happened, but you have never thought carefully about what you lost through that experience. What did you have before the crisis that you feel you no longer have? What did you see for your future then that is no longer possible?

This is not a one-time event, something to check off the list: "I spelled out my loss—now on down the road to healing." You are *beginning* the process here.

My losses are still unraveling. In a store or sitting with friends, without warning, my spirit will ache for a loss that drifts to the surface. Similarly, as the awareness of loss unravels for you over the coming days or months, you might return to this page often.

These bends on your journey cannot be dictated. The way loss drifts to the surface is organic. It is volatile and it is quiet. Sometimes intentional and sometimes unexpected, the sense of loss is, above all, real—and it is right. It is your story. It has worth. It is valuable enough to record.

As often as you discover these layers of truth, return to this bend in the road and listen to your responses as you contemplate these questions:

What was once here that is now gone?

What has been taken from me that I did not willingly give?

What empty places do I see . . . or sense . . . or feel?

What do I reach out to grasp, only to find that it is no longer there?

What might have been possible, but no longer is?

29
EMOTIONS: A TANGLED MESS

It took courage for you to look, to see, to *acknowledge your loss . . . the absence of something.* This is a step forward as we work our way toward *mourning the loss.* As we come to this part of the path and approach the next bend in the road, however, I feel it necessary to forewarn you about a real possibility.

You see, the way the taproot of loss branches out and blossoms into expression is *through emotion*—feelings of all shapes and colors. Feelings of loss can stir up other feelings. One emotion leads to another, which ignites another and another, until soon, we are unsure of where we began. In fact, we often end up blaming a totally unrelated experience for the emotion that is drawing its strength from the distant, deep root of *loss.* For example, perhaps, we have suffering and pain related to a marriage relationship. This loss of relationship can manifest itself in something as simple as frustration about waiting to be seated in a restaurant. Is the source of that frustration truly waiting? Or is it because of our observation that all around us are happy couples enjoying their time together? Loss is the *source* of many emotional responses.

Now that you have started your conversation with loss—you acknowledge that something is gone, that something was taken from you without your permission and outside your control—the mourning process can begin and it may bring intense emotion with it. Once again, we hear that haunting question, "How do you feel?"

One day, as I was turning a skein of yarn into a ball of yarn, I dropped everything. I retrieved it all and attempted to continue, adjusting this piece here and that one there, until I realized that what I held in my hands was a tangled mess. I spent time weaving the yarn in and out of loops and snares. There was no pattern or path that I could easily follow. I would follow one strand and attempt to pull it out of the fray. It would look promising until I realized it was wrapped around another portion of yarn and was dragging that entanglement along with it. It seemed that whenever I thought I had loosed it, there was yet another tangle, another unexpected knot.

That is how we often feel in the midst of our conversation with loss. It is as if we're trying to navigate a tangled pile of emotions. One minute we might feel we're getting somewhere, and the next minute we realize there is yet another mess to sort out. Or, one minute we feel rejection, and the next we actually feel relief. One day we feel lonely, and the next day we distrust anyone who tried to help.

Just as untangling my pile of yarn was a delicate, tedious process, so is the process of untangling our emotions. It's a hands-on project! Eventually, as I loosened my frustrated grip and stopped tugging and pulling, the yarn also began to loosen and I was able to follow a pathway in and out of the entanglement. We each have our own unique tangle of grief and emotion. If we identity some of the strands of loss within our tangle and follow their pathways, they will eventually lead us out of the mess through the process of healthy mourning. Let's take this idea with us to the next bend in the road.

A BEND IN THE ROAD

DISCOVERING
THE EMOTIONS OF LOSS

Take some time to consider the image of tangled yarn on the next page.[1] Look carefully at the words and then think about your own feelings and emotions. It is healthy to honestly admit to real emotions. Perhaps, they sound something like,

> *Yes, I sometimes feel bitter.*
>
> *Yes, I have been angry.*
>
> *Yes, I dread the next day, and the next, and the next.*
>
> *Yes, I regret . . .*

Whatever it is, say it aloud. Speak the words. Speak the emotion. But set aside responses like,

> *I shouldn't . . .*
>
> *I don't want to . . .*
>
> *If anyone knew . . .*

As I went through life, it was never my intention to become comfortable or familiar with such emotions as these. Yet, I am learning that familiarity with my response to suffering will not destroy me. I am safe, even in honestly owning my own bitterness, rage, loneliness—or joy.

You are safe too.

The image of the tangled yarn will help you to gently connect the pathway from *identifying your loss* to *mourning your loss.* Color or shade the spaces that relate to emotions you feel as you think about your loss. Add additional emotions to the empty spaces as needed.

---

[1] Dr. H. Norman Wright initiated the idea of a "ball of emotions" as a way to express the emotions of grief. The illustration used here is my own version.

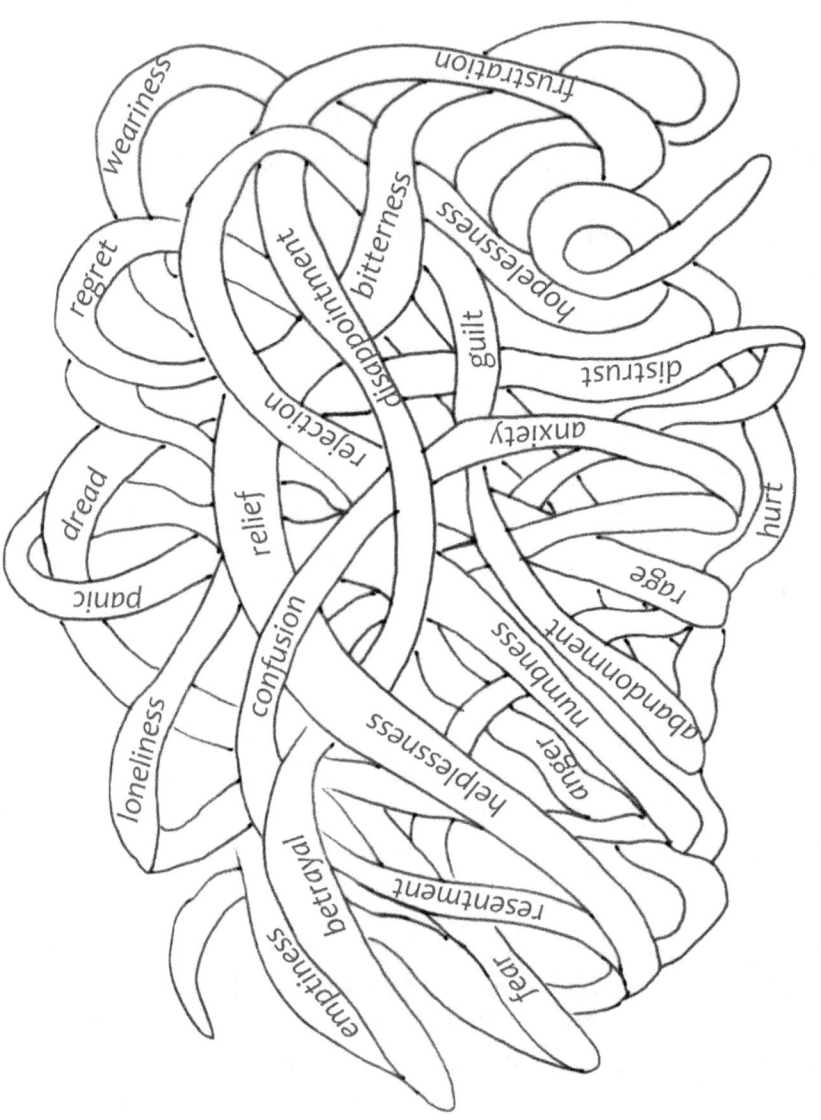

30
MOURNING LOSS

Loss.

Our spirits feel the *absence*. Our bodies feel the *absence*. The emotions of that loss are real and complex.

True loss cries out to be grieved. You may have been told that grieving stirs up unnecessary pain. Maybe you have felt that to grieve is to complain or be dissatisfied. Perhaps, you have been told that if we truly trust God, we will not grieve or feel loss.

This is *absolutely not true.*

To understand this, we must invite Him into the conversation. Along the journey, you have heard references to the Creator, to the One who is on this journey with you. Some of you might not yet acknowledge or welcome Him, let alone trust Him. If that is you, I only ask that you allow me to share a bit of His story, because He and I—and maybe even you—have a few things in common.

Our companion, Jesus, gives us permission to grieve by having done so Himself. Jesus felt loss. Jesus grieved for that loss.

Listen to a part of His story: One of Jesus's dear friends, Lazurus, died. Jesus knew all the details surrounding His friend's death, but Jesus was also fully aware that He, *Himself*, was going to bring His friend, Lazarus, back to life that very day! Still, knowing all of these details, notice how He responded when He saw the pain that was consuming Lazarus's friends and family: "Jesus wept" (John 11:35).

Real tears, welling up out of real loss, flowing from a heart that connected intimately with the pain of others.

Jesus *felt the loss* of Lazarus, His friend. Jesus *felt the loss* of Lazarus's family and loved ones. He knew they were *feeling the absence* of their brother and friend. Jesus *felt the pain* that death brings. He did not tell Himself and everyone standing at the grave, "Put on a brave face; there is no reason for sorrow."

Jesus was profoundly aware of the loss—even with the imminent promise of resurrection! He *embraced the grief* of this loss and *expressed it openly.*

> He did not hide it.

> He did not rebuke it.

> He did not label it as weakness.

Jesus was comfortable *feeling the emotion* and *allowing the overflow of that emotion to be expressed and seen.*

And this was not the only time when Jesus expressed His feelings of loss. On the night Jesus was arrested, He was praying to His Father because He knew the betrayal and the physical and emotional suffering that was upon Him. Listen:

> Then Jesus went with his disciples to a place called Gethsemane, and he said to them, "Sit here while I go over there and pray . . . " Then He said to them, "My soul is overwhelmed with sorrow to the point of death. Stay here and keep watch with me." (Matthew 26:36, 38)

Jesus grieved at the events that were to come. Did you hear the words that He used to describe His sorrow?

> *Overwhelmed. To the point of death.*

Jesus felt loss from the friends and followers who would betray Him, from those who would run away rather than stand with Him in His pain. He felt the loss of those who should publicly recognize Him and instead turn on Him and cry out for His death. Loss upon loss befell—even the Son of God. He grieved to the point that "his sweat was like drops of blood falling to the ground" (Luke 22:44)

The heaviness of loss presses in on our physical bodies, provoking them to respond in unusual and sometimes violent ways. Jesus must have felt a great heaviness of loss and sorrow for His physical body to respond in such a powerful way.

Suffering planted the seed of loss in Jesus's life. That seed came to life and was expressed in actions and in words that we can understand. So, the reality is that we can connect with Him in loss—because He first connected with us in loss.

The experience and expression of suffering are prominent in God's Word.

> There is a time for everything, and a season for every activity under the heavens: . . . a time to weep and a time to laugh, *a time to mourn* and a time to dance. (Ecclesiastes 3:1,4)

There is a time for us to experience and express the loss—even loss that can seemingly overwhelm us to the point of death. *There is a time* to stop and feel and express. During this time it is neither wise nor advisable to rush blindly down the road in a desperate effort to escape.

When we grieve, we declare the existence of the suffering. When we grieve, we open a channel for cleansing.

***

I considered ending the chapter here, but I could not imagine leaving you without some reassurance in your grief. So, here it is: When we grieve, we step onto a path where we can encounter *comfort*.

True comfort. Not platitudes. Not sweet sayings. Comfort that touches our soul.

Where can we receive such comfort? There is but One who offers it: "The Father of compassion and the God of all comfort, who comforts us in all our troubles" (2 Corinthians 1:3-4).

God wants us to communicate our sorrow and pain to Him. In fact, His compassion is how He wants to be known by you!

As we approach our next profound bend in the road—to intentionally mourn the loss we identified—we will need a safety net. We will need assurance of our value. We will need release from the burden that we must somehow deny pain and prove our strength. We will need confidence that what we are about to do is acceptable, right, and good for us.

This is why I encourage you to invite our trustworthy traveling companion into this experience. If He is not with us, we have no safety net. We have no assurance. We have no confidence. We have no real comfort.

Without Him, we cast our precious words and thoughts into the air and we know not where they land. Without Him, we confess our pain into the emptiness, which consumes it without response.

But how does this trusted companion respond to our tears? Perhaps, you have been rebuked for your tears. Perhaps, like me, your tears have at times brought derisive laughter and anger from another. Be assured, God's response to your pain does not incite fear or embarrassment. So, what does it include? What happens to your tears of grief when you express them to Him? Are they discarded, unnoticed?

No, instead, God responds to you as He did to Hezekiah: "I have heard your prayer and seen your tears" (2 Kings 20:5). Or, listen to the way David accorded God's response: "Record my misery; list my tears on your scroll—are they not in your record? (Psalm 56:8) In another passage, David wrote,

> I am worn out from my groaning. All night long I flood my bed with weeping and drench my couch with tears . . . the LORD has heard my weeping." (Psalm 6:6,8)

God, our traveling companion, captures and protects all that we share. Nothing is missed or disregarded. Nothing is left on the floor to be swept away.

Your tears are not unheeded. Your tears are not set aside. Quite the contrary, your tears are part of the story—precious and valuable. God reaches for them, holds them, and keeps a record of them in His book.

Quiet your heart and listen:

> He heals the brokenhearted and binds up their wounds. (Psalm 147:3)
>
> The LORD is close to the brokenhearted and saves those who are crushed in spirit. (Psalm 34:18)

God reveals His compassionate heart by how He sees us: the brokenhearted, the crushed in spirit.

That sounds like One who grasps what the suffering has done to your heart, your spirit, and your soul. That sounds like One who knows your pain and is giving you freedom to *feel* those very emotions.

God not only gives you permission to mourn; He also *feels* the pain in your grieving. He puts Himself in your place:

> For we do not have a high priest who is unable to empathize with our weaknesses . . . Let us then approach God's throne of grace with confidence, so that we may receive mercy and find grace to help us in our time of need. (Hebrews 4:15-16)

As you round the bend, this sweet companion will not stay on the side of the road and shout instructions and nice sayings to you. Can you see Him as He comes close? As He opens His arms? As He turns His ear toward you, leaning in to grasp every detail, every hesitating whisper, every incomplete thought?

A BEND IN THE ROAD,
MOURNING MY LOSS

So, here we are. We have come to the next part of the journey—to intentionally mourn the loss. (Maybe through our discussion, it has already begun.) But, how?

Dear friend, there is no prescribed path of mourning.

Tears. Words. Writing. Quietness. These are only a beginning.

I have mourned while sitting on the rocks at the edge of the sea, shouting my pain to the heavens.

I have mourned quietly sitting in the forest, uttering nothing but my broken sighs. I have mourned by writing my loss and placing it in the fire.

I have mourned by returning to the place of pain, forcing myself to remember and then release it.

And each time, I had my safety net in place. My trusted companion was present, reaching out for me in my pain, counting my tears, binding my wounds, and giving freedom and value to my sorrow.

You will also find your path. You will know when you do. Open yourself to it, but don't force it. My encouragement to you is when an emotion of loss wells up from deep inside you, follow it.

Your willingness to follow through will not be fruitless. It will not be taken for granted. But your open expression of loss will require your trust . . .

- *that this is a good thing for you to do;*
- *that to open your soul and expose your pain, even into an empty room, will not be met with contempt or indifference;*
- *that your words of truth will not fall unnoticed and be scattered about on the floor, or even worse, rise up to accuse you in your moment of vulnerability;*
- *that you will not be overwhelmed with sorrow to the point of death.*

This is a time when you might involve someone else on your journey. Perhaps you can tell one trusted person that you are taking this intentional time to grieve. Regardless of whether you tell another person, however, I encourage you to include the perfect companion in the process, for He is the One of all comfort.

Carefully ponder the following prompts and see where they may lead:

What words come?

What expressions of pain? How do I describe the loss?

How has my physical body shown evidence of the grief?

What doubts and questions rise up?

How will I mourn?

Truthfully   *Openly*   *With Trust*

31
CASTING

Here we stand.

We have opened our hearts. We are holding our grief. We are experiencing our emotions.

Where do we go next?

I am committed to being honest with you, to speaking the truth of my journey. And so, I have nowhere to lead you than to the only One who has been able to meet me at that place—that place where I find myself with an . . .

open heart,

raw wounds,

outstretched hands running over with grief,

emotions churning, tumbling, and grasping for attention.

Who is this One who, with confidence, offers this profound gift of comfort and support? We have spoken of Him previously as Creator and Companion. Now we will also get to know Him as Good Shepherd, the One who cares for us. We will continue to know more of Him as He connects with us in the layers of our suffering and the tapestry of our lives.

He is personal and intentional in His interactions with each of us. From the darkness, I hear these words: *Cast your cares on Me, and I will sustain you.* Yes, He says,

Cast your cares on the LORD, and he will sustain you. (Psalm 55:22)

The sadness, anger, fear, loneliness, despair—these are all *cares*. All the emotions of grief and loss are *cares*. The physical responses are also cares. To *cast* our cares on the LORD is to put our cares on Him. He does not intend for us to carry those cares, that grief, by ourselves. They are too heavy. The burden is too great.

God speaks, saying: *"Give them to Me."*

Oh, but it is stronger than that. To *cast* is to *throw*. Picture a fisherman *casting* his line into the sea. He pulls his arm back and tosses it out with strength—away from himself and into the deep.

This particular invitation carries with it a profound promise, one that we desperately need right now.

> THE INVITATION: *"Cast your cares on Me."*

> THE PROMISE: *"I will sustain you."*

Have you ever tried to physically throw something that is very heavy? That action can set us *off-balance*. The same is true when we attempt to cast off our heavy burden of grief and suffering. This action can be unsettling, even destabilizing. We have grown accustomed to the weight of the pain and the guilt. But when we cast that burden onto our Companion, He sustains and supports us through the imbalance of the weight, as it shifts away from us and onto Him.

> THE REALITY: *God is able to absorb our grief.*

He is able to *absorb* all of it. To *absorb* is to take in, or soak up. Think of a sponge. If you place a dry sponge in water, it soaks up the water. The problem with a sponge is that it can get so full of water that it cannot absorb any more. At that point, it simply sits there and becomes overwhelmed by the deluge, virtually of no further use.

But God is able to absorb every last drop of our loss and pain. He will never say that He can take no more. He will never be overwhelmed by the deluge of our suffering.

Do you see this wonderful picture?

God sees our cares, our grief, and our loss.

He tells us to throw that grief onto Him.

He supports and carries us through the
    emotional awareness.

And He absorbs all that we can give to Him.

It is never too much. And He does not return it to us.

I have experienced loss and uninvited suffering. And even though God is familiar to me and I trust Him, there were times when I felt fear, guilt, rejection, anger, and pain. My feelings would threaten to overwhelm me.

One day, I went to a place of safety to be alone with God. I went to the sea. I walked far out onto the jetty and stood, with the waves crashing on the rocks around me. I opened my heart, my hands, and my mouth, and I cast my loss and my grief onto God.

Some emotions came out in a shout from deep inside, momentarily throwing me off balance. My Companion held me safe.

How does that kind of safety feel? It may be different for each of us. For me, I sensed that my pain was no longer going to carry me over the edge into that deep place of despair that I had once felt. I knew that I was not going to lose touch with reality. When my expression of suffering came out of me, I knew it would not sweep back over me in a counterattack. Why? Because God was absorbing it away from me. And as He absorbed, He held me in check so that I could stand with a tenacity and courage that was beyond my own.

Many emotions also came out of me as tears from the very depth of my being. Initially, some were almost violent, but then they eventually diminished to a resigned whimper. God knew those tears; He kept record of each one.

And as I stood there, I was aware that God was absorbing all of it—every minute detail.

> All the loss.
> All the pain.
> All the betrayal.
> All the anger.
> All the disappointment.

He took it all. I don't know where He stored it. I just know that He knew what to do with it.

Does this mean that I will never experience such awareness of pain again? No. The emotions still come, often when I least expect them. Sorrow washes over me. Painful memories bring more tears. But I have found that each time the need for casting comes, I remember who is on the journey with me. Once again, I need Him to absorb and hold me safe while I cast my cares. Each time, He absorbs all that I cast *away from me and onto Him.*

So, as time goes on, the grief of loss still comes, but it becomes less terrifying and less overwhelming.

We are not to ignore the loss.

We are not to hide the emotions that speak for the loss.

Identify the loss. Mourn for it. Express it.

Then cast it . . .

onto the One who can absorb it all. He knows what to do with it.

Where will you go? Where is your place to cast?

As soon as you feel comfortable, or at least determined enough, find a safe place where you can cast . . . out and away from yourself. Discover the One who is able to absorb it all.

Whatever you cast will never be too offensive.

Never too broken.

Never too confusing, jumbled, or illogical.

Never too intense or too much.

Never more than He can absorb.

Record your responses and thoughts here.

RESPONDING TO DESPAIR

Suffering is real.
But the accusation "all is lost,"
that rises out of the resulting trauma,
is untruth.

32
WHAT IS LEFT OF ME?

At one point during my crisis, as I was facing the loss and the reality of *life as it is now*, I found myself on my knees, crying out, "What is left of me? What is left of Susan?"

It was a desperately empty feeling. I was confused. I was afraid. It seemed that "Susan" had been swept away into the overwhelming deluge of pain, accusation, betrayal, and guilt.

What is left of me? Perhaps this question has drifted into your thoughts while you were identifying loss. Maybe you have kept that concern buried deep inside, fearful to even ask the question.

A common threat that invades our thoughts is, "ALL is lost. You cannot survive. You have been consumed by your suffering. *You are undone.*"

Remember, suffering is real. But, the *accusations* that rise out of the resulting trauma are often *untruth*. Our healing is dependent on our discernment of the truth and the untruth.

The intent for this journey is to experience the moment, not to run ahead on the path. However, this is one of the few times that I will encourage you *a few steps further down the road.*

I have discovered that Susan still *is*. Yes, there are parts of me that were literally burned up, purified through suffering. There are parts of me that are gone just because circumstances have changed.

But, one morning, my precious traveling Companion shared a truth with me that I desperately needed to hear:

> [My] eyes saw [your] unformed substance; in [My] book were written,
> every one of them, the days that were formed for [you], when as yet there
> was none of them. (Psalm 139:16 ESV)

"What," I questioned, "is my substance?" It seemed to carry such depth—beyond my physical body.

"Your substance," I heard Him reply to my spirit, "is that which I created of you, that which can never be destroyed. Your substance is the Susan that I see and know and love and value. Your substance is your story that I have written and preserved in my book. Your substance is what has survived the fire, because I have held it close and protected it."

Yes! I finally felt freedom to accept that *who I really am*—is *who I am still.* In fact, in many ways I am *more me* than ever before. There have been times that I had attempted to be what I thought I *should* be, or what I thought others wanted me to be. There were times I was carried away by a need to define my identity only to discover that the enticement was empty. But now, pretense is gone; chains are broken. I no longer must fight to keep the worst from happening. It has already happened.

My suffering is part of my substance. My days of pain are written in God's book, because they are valuable. But any actions of others that caused that pain—*those are not part of my substance.* I need not carry those forward with me. There were circumstances that held me captive, but they did not destroy my substance. The labels that others might have placed on me are not the words written in His book. But my substance, which God saw *before anyone* else *could*—that *me* still is! And the same is true for you.

Even after all you have lost . . . here you are; the substance of you.

There is no bend in the road for this part of the journey—just a truth to bring up as a shield when trauma throws its darts of accusation and threats of annihilation.

You are.

You have not been destroyed

You have not been consumed.

You—the substance of you—exists eternally.

And you are valuable.

In you, the brokenhearted . . . is beauty.

In you, who mourn . . . is beauty.

In you, who have carried a spirit of despair . . . is beauty.

The evil intentions of this world are determined to destroy true beauty.

Your suffering, at first glance,

appears to have done the same.

But, as you journey through suffering . . .

you are not destroyed, but purified.

Your story has purpose.

Your pain has value.

You are a planting of the LORD

who displays the splendor of the Living God.

He has sent me [Jesus] to bind up the brokenhearted, to proclaim
freedom for the captives . . . to comfort all who mourn, and provide
for those who grieve . . . to bestow on them a crown of beauty
instead of ashes, the oil of joy instead of mourning, and a garment
of praise instead of a spirit of despair. They will be called . . . a
planting of the LORD for the display of his splendor.

Isaiah 61:1–3

34
A NEW VILLAIN

One day, a few years after my crisis event, I was experiencing a full onslaught of painful emotion. It was washing over me, the memories crowding into my mind, demanding center stage. Yes—those emotions come back, even years later. Anniversaries of the event are times of particular vulnerability.

This time, it began with strong physical reactions: the inability to eat, nausea, and pain. These symptoms were not unusual. And then it broke forth—emotions, cries, words spewing up from some dark place, much of it sounding very familiar:

> "How could this have happened?"
>
> "How is this possible?"
>
> "I am so angry. I hate it. I hate . . . "
>
> and then it came, rushing out, without any warning
>
> "I hate *me. I hate myself*."

LORD, have mercy, what was happening? This part of the journey had taken an unexpected turn. And yet it came with such reality, clarity, and vehemence.

Looking directly at me, the object of my emotion, was a villain who was new to me but had a familiar face. This unexpected villain who had entered my story was *me*.

Oh, I had been haunted by the awareness of my part in pain—in my own life and in the lives of others—many times. I had questioned myself. But now, degrading accusation, and powerful guilt came in one crushing blow. It was almost more than I could bear.

I could have . . . I should have . . . Why didn't I . . . ?

It's me. I'm the one. I'm the one who carries the responsibility for the pain.

Angry, hateful responses flowed out of me and then unexpectedly washed back over me with tsunami-like power. The peace that had settled over my life was torn apart and threatened by accusations and loathing—from the one source I had not expected it.

And now I was faced with a looming darkness. A darkness that threatened to pull me under. Run away. Give in. Withdraw.

I will not tell you that this new pain resolved itself easily or quickly. Resolution is still an ongoing process. But I am compelled to open this conversation to acknowledge the possibility that you are undergoing a similar experience in your own life. There will likely come a time when, with some validity—or with no justification at all—you accuse *yourself*. It might sneak up on you quietly or erupt suddenly and show no mercy. But when it happens, know this: you are not alone in that place.

I suppose that we all *could have* avoided some detail of the suffering—*if only* it had happened under other conditions. However, we must be very careful of entertaining *could-haves* and *if-onlys,* because they can consume and destroy us.

This self-accusation is another layer of the effects of trauma. In fact, it can be one of the most difficult layers. What has made it so difficult for me is that mixed in with all of the invalid accusations is the awareness that there have been times in my life when I really could have done some things differently—and that those slight or significant changes would have made a difference in my life and in the lives of others. That realization brings pain that cuts deeper than anything I have ever experienced.

Perhaps, such a realization is another form of loss. The cry of our hearts is to be wise, to make the right decisions, to protect ourselves and others. And then we are faced with the reality that, at some moment in time, we *did not* do these things. Most likely, the mistakes were unintentional and often the result of valid and legitimate choices we made in the moment— and yet, those decisions may have opened doors through which evil came.

It is possible that someone is blaming and accusing us. It is possible that we are blaming ourselves. Either way, we feel betrayed by our own part in the narrative. Even if we are not truly to blame, we accuse ourselves without logic: we should have been wiser, stronger, more careful.

Now, quickly following on the heels of accusation, is another attacker. *Shame* creeps over us for what we didn't do, the decisions we did and didn't make, the actions we did and didn't take. It can get to the point that we find ourselves cowering under our self-imposed guilt.

We might feel shame for being in the situation, shame that our family members or our marriage did such and such a thing. We might feel shame for being so vulnerable, broken, or a victim. Shame that we couldn't fix things. Shame that we couldn't avoid something. Shame that we couldn't undo what had already been done.

Accusation. Guilt. Shame. What do we do with them?

The answer for me comes with brutal honesty: *I feel them.*

A small part of me would like for someone to talk me out of it.

Another part of me feels the need to stay in the suffering, in some way paying for the pain. (Someone should pay, right? Maybe it should be me.)

Yet another part of me pushes back, because to feel any responsibility for the trauma feels like I am exonerating the true source of the pain.

Have you experienced this struggle? Here is what I discovered through this particular bend in the road.

If we could have recognized the signs—locked a door, moved people out of the house more quickly, asked more questions, spoken to someone more clearly, avoided a situation—or done whatever we wish we would have done differently, we can say, "I'm sorry." We can speak the words to another person. We can speak the words to ourselves. We can speak the words to Jesus, who feels our pain.

Further, it is possible to be sorry about some part of an event, without taking on the burden of the entire experience.

And here is a final bit of advice to you (and to me): Recognize the truly impossible I-should-haves, and set them aside.

Let us take these ideas with us into our next bend in the road.

Are you ready to acknowledge and pour out your hidden sorrow, buried accusations, and hidden feelings of guilt—to give words to them?

This bend in the road is an opportunity to speak aloud or record in writing the self-accusation that haunts you. If it is there, continuing to hide it will only increase the pain. On the other hand, every time you bring a hidden threat into the light, you break its hold on you—which moves you further down the path of healing.

Listen carefully, though: This exercise is about acknowledging the guilt and shame that plague you *in order to take back its control.* This is *not* an exercise in wallowing in guilt or dwelling on your inability to prevent or fix the suffering. This is *not* about taking responsibility or attempting to pay for the sorrow through your own pain. This is about freeing your mind from the clutches of trauma as it attempts to destroy peace, hope, and forward movement. It is a way for you to begin to recognize the tactics of pain, which attempts to consume and control you.

We can acknowledge that the self-accusations are there without embracing and nurturing them. If we embrace them, they will continue to haunt and threaten us, growing in intensity and spiraling into unreasonable conclusions about who we are. We end up thinking, *I am a bad person because I . . .* But this kind of thinking is not healthy. It only pulls us deeper into hiding our shame, suppressing our story, and submitting to the negative effects of the suffering.

We must express regret, extend an apology if necessary, and then offer ourselves grace. A wise counselor said to me, "You cannot go back and pass judgment on yourself *then* based on the information that you have *now*." Maybe you need to hear that wisdom as well. This truth applies to past and, even, to current suffering.

The bottom line: Shame has no place in our healing journey.

But by speaking openly and honestly about the sadness and regret you feel, you can begin to take back control. Be a good traveling companion. Listen carefully. Don't undermine the emotion. Listen to the story. And then, be ready to reassure.

Sometimes, when you hear yourself say your thoughts out loud, you realize how unacceptable the self-accusations are. You know what you would say to someone else who spoke those same words about themselves. You hear the truthful response you would give to reassure them.

Remember that you can speak the words to yourself, to another person, or to your Creator, who feels your pain. Also remember that it is possible to be sorry about some part of an event, without taking on the burden of the entire experience.

To cast the first unspoken words out into the air or onto paper, it might help to start with the words, "I regret . . . " or "I'm sad that . . . " You might also use one or more of the prompts below as a springboard.

I wish I could have done this differently:

I am sad that I was not able to keep this from happening:

I am sad that I did not protect myself from this thing or in this way:

I regret that I did not respond in this way:

Use the space on the following page to write your own words:

I...

COURAGE TO MOVE FORWARD

*The pain from suffering
can become comfortable,
like an ill-fitting pair of shoes
that has become familiar.
But when you courageously
take the steps anyway,
the narrative of your story
begins to come to life in unexpected ways.*

35
RESOLUTION

Could it be? Is it possible, that we are moving toward resolution?

We have looked at our suffering full on. We have considered the ways that trauma deceives us. We have acknowledged our losses and begun the process of mourning them. The threat of suffering is now weakening because we have revealed its negative tactics. We have not taken the easy way; we have stayed on the path and taken every bend in the road.

We are discovering that resolution is not a straight line.

Resolution moves forward and upward

> and then hesitates and takes a backward step;

> > it even goes downward for a moment,

> > > before moving forward once again.

To bring resolution is to acknowledge that the event happened, that the immediate danger has come to an end, and that we are not going to actively live in fear of that danger. We accept the reality of the crisis but we refuse to live under its control.

Be encouraged. You have made progress, growing stronger and more courageous. In truth, you are *making peace* with the crisis event.

It is quite possible that this does not sit well with you. "Make peace?" Even those words trigger a defense mechanism that makes us want to shout, "No!"

I hear you. To *make peace* feels like we are caving in. But stay with me. Let's come at it from another perspective.

We discussed earlier that suffering often leads to trauma. We identified trauma as that time when the suffering takes control of many parts of our lives and keeps us from functioning in a healthy way. Many of us have lived with trauma for years, continually under its threat. And in many ways, suffering and trauma have overpowered our identities, changing how we see ourselves.

So, we must learn to have a different relationship with suffering. We must *come to peace* with the suffering, which is another way of saying the following:

> I acknowledge that the suffering happened. I am no longer trying to rewrite the story.

> I acknowledge that the crisis event changed things in my life. I am no longer trying to recreate my life as it was.

> I mourn the losses that have resulted from the suffering. I am no longer trying to deny them.

> I acknowledge that the suffering is now a part of me. I am no longer trying to deny or hide it.

Now, here comes another emotional, perhaps hard-to-swallow, word: *concede.*

To *concede* is to "admit that something is true after first denying or resisting it."

We usually have a negative response to the word, *concede.* We liken it to "giving in." And, in truth, that is exactly what we need to do—we need to concede, or *give in,* to the reality of the suffering. We need to fully and completely, without reservation, admit that it is true.

The pain. The loss. The betrayals. The rejection. The physical and emotional undoing. The scars. It is all true—in *my* life. In *your* life. It is part of our story.

We have spent days, months, sometimes even years, pushing back against this reality. Fighting with it in our minds—all the what-ifs,

> the should-haves

> the shouldn't-haves,

> the I-wish-I-wouldn't-haves.

We have used resources we did not possess. We have lost sleep. We have told ourselves untruth. We have expended enormous amounts of energy and effort trying to defend ourselves against the reality of this horrific event.

Now, it's time to concede. It's time to make peace. It's time to give suffering its identity. Yet, the next step of resolution must quickly follow—it now becomes time to establish boundaries.

We must learn to say, "That's enough."

My father came from a large family of four girls and six boys. As you can imagine, sometimes life was chaotic. My father told the story of one such time. The boys were wrestling, and as their rough-and-tumble play continued to build in intensity, the boundaries got pushed—and suddenly, the front room window was broken. What followed was my grandfather's authoritative and firm response in Swiss German: "*Das ist genug!*" meaning, "That's enough!" to which the boys quickly responded.

Suffering is a reality. It should not be hidden. It is expected to disturb the peace, but sometimes it goes too far and pushes the boundaries. These are the times we must say with authority, "That's enough!"

Essentially, we must say,

> *Suffering, I give full recognition of your identity.*
>
> *I know you are there. I acknowledge you.*
>
> *But I will not live under your control.*
>
> *So, we are now going to come to an agreement.*

The important and critical distinction of this agreement that you make with your suffering, compared with most other agreements, is that you alone get to write it. You get to dictate the terms and draw the lines.

Yes, it is time for a bend in the road.

A BEND IN THE ROAD
RESOLUTION

Use the empty space below to create an agreement with your suffering. Write about your concession to suffering. You might also want to include some boundaries.

Be detailed. And be honest—to yourself and to your suffering.

Here are some examples that may help you to give words to your thoughts:

I concede.

Suffering, I give you full recognition of your identity.

I know you are there. I acknowledge you. But I will not live under your control.

I know you have changed things in this area of my life. I feel it and acknowledge it. But I will not allow you to obstruct my forward movement in this area of my future.

We must come to peace with each other. So, we are now going to come to an agreement.

36
A STRANGE COMFORTABLENESS

We have been working hard . . .

>opening doors that we previously kept closed,

>feeling emotions that we had hoped to avoid,

>expressing our thoughts without backing down.

With each bend in the road, we have gained strength and courage.

Is there still pain? Of course! Is there still fear and hesitation? Yes!

However, now, you are more able to have a conversation with suffering *on your terms*. You have become more comfortable with the evidence of suffering in your story. And you have become more familiar with the characteristics of trauma—better able to recognize its attempts to manipulate you and to hold you in a place of confusion and upheaval.

You have become more capable in these areas because the primary focus of our journey to this point has been to look into the face of the pain that torments us, to recognize it, and to become familiar with its tactics as it attempts to consume us. Doing these things was necessary for our healing. If we never took on the challenge, fear would continue to keep us paralyzed.

But as we come to our next bend in the road, we also come to a crossroad: we must make a choice. The reality and inevitability of healing is that at some point, each of us makes this choice, whether we consciously intend to or not.

Either we . . .

1. take on the identity of our trauma, believe the lie that our value and story are tarnished, give in to the fear of further disappointment, and choose to live life in pain;

>or

2. acknowledge our pain, accepting the suffering as part of our story, and then open our very souls to new possibilities and the remainder of our journey.

Choosing the second option is not as easy as it sounds. And many of you know this.

Pain and suffering can so easily become who we are that we often often find it difficult to move away from the trauma. Suffering, pain, upheaval, despair—not one of us longs for these in our lives, yet, as strange as it might sound, they can become so familiar to us that we start to feel comfortable having them around.

We understand the idea of *becoming familiar* with something. We have become familiar with the tactics of trauma so that we can recognize and lessen its threatening grasp on us. But, now that we add the idea of becoming *comfortable* with it, we ask, "How can something so horrible become *comfortable*?"

The comfortableness comes because we have lived with the suffering for a long time. We have adjusted our lives to it. We have learned to walk in a particular way to accommodate it. We are familiar with the pain. So, the choice must be made:

1. Will we continue to adjust and avoid in order to survive?

2. Or will we consider a new possibility of moving forward?

Making this choice is a challenge that will take courage.

My intense hope is that I have gained some trust from you throughout this journey, for what I am about to say could be interpreted as uncaring and harsh, even accusatory. As we move forward, please know that my vision for us is to break the power that trauma holds on us. If we are to do this, however, we must shine light on the deceptions and uncover the traps. We do this by asking ourselves difficult questions and being honest with ourselves about how we are feeling and what we are thinking.

In that same line of thinking, consider the following question and the responses that follow. Do any of the responses seem to ring true for you, even if just a little? Please be honest with yourself, but also be gentle with yourself. Remember your progress on this journey so far, which reflects your strength. Also know that, although each of us experiences our own unique narrative, we all face many of the same challenges, as well. Thus, we are all asking and reflecting on this difficult question together:

How does my suffering feel familiar, even *comfortable*? How does a life *outside* of my trauma feel *un*comfortable?

* In some odd way, I know what to expect from my suffering. I know the emotions it will bring; even the ache is familiar to me.
* I find some level of comfort in my pain, in the fact that I have been wronged.
* If I begin to move away from my trauma, people will expect more from me; they will think I am healed. They will move on and expect me to do the same.
* My trauma has become a "reason" for negative responses to others. My accountability—or lack of responsibility—rests in the pain inflicted on me.
* If I begin to live outside of my trauma, the instrument of my pain will think I have forgiven or passed beyond the suffering.
* If I do not hold my trauma as my identity, anyone who I am in a new relationship with will not know my pain; they will not know my struggle and my story.
* If I begin to release my trauma, it will minimize the severity of the initial event.
* I feel guilty when stepping beyond my trauma, because others were hurt, too. Joy and hope in my life will cause others to think that I don't remember their pain.

Our minds can come up with all sorts of accusations against us, ways to keep us under the control of our past hurts. So, it is important that we understand that what we are not talking about is not putting the suffering in a box under the bed.

We are not saying we will never talk about these events or experience their effects again. We are speaking only about being *directionally correct,*

We want to move from 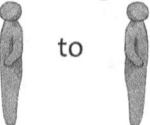 to

And ultimately, we want to move from a paralyzed backward focus to some form of movement forward for the rest of the journey—

        from   to   or even

Think of a dramatic play or a musical. When the actors perform, they are following the words and actions written by the author. These words and actions are contained in the *script.* The actors do not create their own words and actions while they are on the stage; they follow the script that was given to them. No matter how they feel that day, they must express the emotions described in the script.

Now, think of your life like a play. Who is writing the script for you? It can be easy—comfortable—to allow *trauma* to become the writer of the script we follow. When trauma takes this role, no matter what is happening in our lives at the time, our words, emotions, and actions are dictated by the script of suffering. When this happens, we cannot move forward, because we remain under trauma's negative control.

Maybe you're thinking, *It is not comfort, but fear—fear of the future—that holds me back.* Oh, I connect with you in that response. But do you see that in such a response, we give in to the logic of the trauma? We conclude that . . .

    the painful status quo seems safer than the potential discomfort of the future; and

    the familiarity of the present suffering feels safer than the unknown possibilities of the future.

It is time for a deep breath. Time for a bend in the road.

A BEND IN THE ROAD
TO HONESTLY SPEAK THE
FAMILIARITY OF THE SUFFERING THAT HOLDS ME

What about you? What has become comfortable about your story of suffering?

What has threatened you, convinced you to fear, even avoid, moving forward?

What reasons seem logical enough to hold you in place?

As you consider these questions, remember a bit of our etiquette for the journey:

Trust yourself enough to be honest. You might feel tempted to deny the rawness of what comes to the surface. But there will be no healing if you simply repeat the responses dictated in the script of suffering. There will be no forward movement if you simply read the lines as trauma has written them.

And in all things, *speak truth*. Sometimes, it will bring relief. Sometimes, it will sting. Yet, truth, even with its jagged edges, will move you closer to healing. There is freedom in speaking the truth to ourselves.

Now is the safe time and place to express the comfortableness and fear that hold you in place.

As you do, I hope that you find, as I have, that the threat of the "what could happen" loses its horrific persona when I walk past it with courage, even into the unknown.

37
A NEW PAIR OF SHOES

Imagine a pair of shoes that don't fit you well.

Something about them isn't quite right. They cause pain on your little toe and your heel. But you need to keep moving. So, you begin to adjust how your feet hit the ground. You roll them a bit to one side so that the shoes won't rub painfully across your little toes. You put less of your weight on your heels. You might not even realize you are making these adjustments; you are doing them subconsciously in order *to avoid the pain*.

After walking this way for some time, your adjusted stride begins to feel very familiar, almost comfortable. In fact, when you finally buy a new pair of shoes that fit you well, they feel strange at first. You had become so familiar with the way you needed to walk in the ill-fitting shoes in order to avoid the pain that walking correctly now feels almost uncomfortable.

The same thing happens when we learn to "walk" a certain way through suffering. We attempt to keep going, adjusting our stride in whatever way necessary to elude the dull aches, the sharp twinges, or the ever-present tenderness.

We adapt. We avoid. We never give ourselves fully to life, because the weight of doing so increases the pain.

After a while, this adjusted way of living with the negative effects of suffering becomes familiar. So, in the same way that we might feel uncomfortable in a new pair of shoes after adjusting to the old ones, we might also feel some discomfort as we attempt to walk a new pathway—even one that is leading us beyond the control of trauma and toward healing.

This is my way of alerting you that there might be some discomfort ahead, some unfamiliarity . . . but know that your new pair of shoes is waiting and that, with time, they will be a good fit.

38
MOVING FORWARD

So, what is the tipping point to *moving forward*? At what point does the heart become ready?

The tipping point happens when . . .

the pull toward life outweighs the familiarity of our suffering,

our yearning to move forward overpowers the fears and challenges of the future,

the desire to be free is greater than the comfort and ease of despair.

The ease of despair?

Yes. Moving forward takes great effort. It's hard work doing things that feel unnatural. In comparison, remaining in despair takes very little effort. Oh, it is *painful!* It *feels* like work. But the very definition of despair is simply to give in and allow the trauma to hold us under its control.

And yes, there can be something comforting about not being in control. For a time.

Yet, most of us are feeling a stirring inside to break free—to get back control, to go forward. Although we have experienced great pain, most of us don't want to *remain* in that place. And that is when we reach the tipping point.

Reaching that point of readiness and taking the first steps forward is one of those *alone on the journey* moments. The decision is yours. You must want it for yourself. Even the One who travels with you allows this choice to be yours.

Remember that taking the first steps on that new path may feel uncomfortable. Know, also, that you will likely face doubts as you start to move forward:

But my mind is full of memories.

> (We must add new memories.)

But my day is filled with triggers that take me back.

> (We must create new connections and begin to disconnect the old.)

The loss overwhelms me, even though I know there are some good things.

> (We must be overwhelmed by the good things, even though we are aware of the loss.)

But when you take the steps anyway, the narrative of your story begins to come to life in unexpected ways. That's because the moment you decide to move forward is the moment you begin to take control away from the trauma.

We have spoken often about taking the control away from the negative effects of suffering. But what does that mean? What does it look like?

We learned long ago that we cannot control circumstances and people—not in a way that would protect us from all harm and negative impact. In fact, this is a truth we now comprehend very well. Being faced with this reality is likely what caused our pain in the first place. Something happened to us that was out of our control; something intruded into our story without permission.

There may be circumstances that are out of our control, however—*we can put boundaries on the negative effects of our suffering.*

We can speak truth to ourselves.

We can take control over . . .

> where we find our identity.
>
> which direction we look.
>
> how we spend our mind-time.
>
> where we seek comfort.
>
> how we care for ourselves.

Yes, suffering happened to us. It is part of our story. It may have even left scars. We cannot change or control that reality. But it is within our control to keep suffering from becoming our identity. It is also within our control to change our path forward, but first we must make the decision: to step out from under the debilitating threat with which pain first entered our lives.

As you consider the readiness of your heart to make this decision, let's briefly revisit what "moving forward" does not mean. I have heard so many express faulty expectations of the healing process, expectations often distorted by suffering, and these faulty ideas can prevent healing. So, listen carefully—these are things that you should *not* expect as part of the process of moving forward:

- You are not trying to forget the event.
- You are not trying to "think only positive thoughts."
- You are not trying to play a part or turn over a new leaf.
- You are not attempting to put life back together again, the way it was.
- You are not trying to create a new life that excludes the awareness of the past.
- Making forward movement does not mean that you will never again shed tears or shout at the heavens.
- It does not mean that you will restore all relationships.
- It does not mean you won't revisit some of the conversations we have had up to this point.

Forward movement is just that: you are simply making a move forward into life as it is now.

Yes . . . there is *life now*. Possibility. Value. Hope.

Life now . . .

It does not look like *before*, the way we thought life was.

However, it is not consumed with the hurt and brokenness, either.

New growth is starting—even where branches were broken. There is evidence of life and light within and there are new paths leading to new experiences.

Does it sound inviting? Does it sound, perhaps, like an odd mixture of anticipation, doubt, joy, fear, and relief—a little unfamiliar? That is normal. New shoes often feel that way.

My grandson found reading and math to be a particular challenge. It wasn't from lack of determination; but extra time and effort did not bring the results he desired. Then we discovered vision therapy—exercises that trained his eyes to work in sync, to discern correctly, and to process information in a way that was useable. Soon, his eyes were passing relevant truthful messages with confidence to his brain. Problems became solvable. Words now appeared organized into sentences and paragraphs. He discovered a new way of seeing that helped him interpret and interact with the world around him in a healthy, productive way.

Do we need a new way of "seeing"?

As we have discovered, sometimes it feels as if suffering is the only topic of our story, overshadowing everything else in life. If we were asked to portray our life story in an image, we would likely create a picture in which suffering was the focal point. In fact, in some of our pictures, suffering might be the only subject matter depicted!

The image might appear to be like the one below, in which the suffering . . .

overwhelms everything,

colors all aspects of life, and

leaves very little space untouched.

All of our senses, life circumstances, thoughts, and emotions connect to the pain. The event feels like a perpetual attack, and every part of us—body, soul, and spirit—responds in self-defense. The result is that everything feels *negative* in some way.

Superlative and all-inclusive statements headline the conversations we have with others and ourselves:

> "All is lost."
>
> "No one cares."
>
> "Everything is a mess."
>
> "Nothing is turning out the way I expected."
>
> "No one understands."
>
> "Nothing can make this better."
>
> "I will never trust anyone for the rest of my life."

And on and on it goes. We can see no good in anything, because the pain has taken over. Moments of "right" are so overwhelmed by "wrong" that they disappear into the background of our image of life, while the focal point of suffering continues to stand front and center.

But this is not a truthful image. The *truth* is that there is more to our story.

The truth is that suffering disturbs our acceptance of anything good or positive, even about ourselves. Surprisingly, this can even extend so far as to cloud our memories of good things that happened *before* the crisis—things that are completely unrelated. It is as if our body and mind respond so defensively to the attack that they throw out a blanket of protection that covers everything without distinction.

Any acknowledgement of good feels disloyal. Any positive response seems to signal pardon or at least weaken the accountability of the root of the suffering. And *trauma is never satisfied*. It continues to eat away at every part of the good.

Part of moving forward and taking back control from the trauma is uncovering the defenses we've put up against this distortion of truth. To do this, we must give ourselves permission to *remember the good.*

We must acknowledge some positive things in life, but this is much more than simply attempting to look at life with optimism. We are not trying to offset the negative with positive thinking; there is no positive that can undo the negative that has happened! We are also not trying just to make ourselves feel better.

We are, however, intent on recognizing the truth that there is legitimate *good*. The truth that God's hand is at work even when we cannot see Him. God assures us that, even in suffering, He is doing a wonderful work in our lives. And He is with us in our stories—at *every* point of our stories.

Now, we must be careful with this exercise. The idea is not to rearrange the details of the event so we now see evidence of some good. It is also not to surmise what potential good could come from our suffering in the future. It is not wise to devise a brilliant story of God's intention that somehow *validates* our suffering; we are neither capable nor trustworthy enough to discern eternal good.

Following closely on that idea is the reality that *we might not ever be able to identify the good*. But, even when we cannot identify it, *it is there*. We can embrace that truth without attempting to define the good.

In other words, we should not try to *create* a story of good to validate the suffering. Doing so attempts to speak the mind of God without true knowledge. Doing so also tries to balance the crisis events against some form of pretty outcome. In the end, it feels like we are saying that the evil was acceptable in order to accomplish some form of good.

The challenge is *not* to try to find the good—
but to be ready and willing to *recognize it when God reveals it.*

Joseph was able to do that. If you do not know Joseph's story, it is a good read. In the Bible, it appears in the book of Genesis in chapters 37, 39, and 40-45. To summarize, Joseph suffered at the hands of his own brothers along with others who accused him falsely and tried to harm him, imprison him, and take his life. His story includes the following crisis events:

- Experiencing betrayal by family
- Being thrown into unfamiliar surroundings
- Being falsely accused by those who held power
- Enduring physical discomfort and danger
- Having intentional harm inflicted on him by those who were supposed to protect him
- Hiding his identity from family

As we read Joseph's story, we dare not hunt around each negative, attempting to find a positive to offset it. However, if we look at how his story unfolds, we can see the *reality of good*: the events of his suffering moved Joseph into a place of responsibility and influence. When it was all over, Joseph said to those who had tried to harm him,

> You intended to harm me, but God intended it for good to accomplish what is now being done, the saving of many lives. (Genesis 50:20)

Joseph acknowledged that his suffering was real and that intentional harm was aimed in his direction by those he trusted. But, even in *the reality of pain and betrayal*, he was also able to see and speak *the reality of good. Both were present.* His understanding of good, however, came after the fact, as more of the picture came clear.

God will not always reveal the good to us as clearly as He did to Joseph. But God *does* insist on the *reality* that good will be seen in the eternal and heavenly realm. Even in the midst of suffering, He is working for the good of His kingdom and for *our* good, personally:

> And we know that in all things God works for the good of those who love him, who have been called according to his purpose. (Romans 8:28)

This verse does not say that the evil that was done to us was or is *good*. God says that He is able to *bring good*—even out of the painful events in your story.

> The *good* in every story is that God says there will be good
> *from an eternal perspective.*

This possibility stretches our way of thinking. The truth of good, even in the presence of suffering, is a reality that brings assurance and allows us to move forward. It allows us to *see the potential of good*, even in the midst and the aftermath of destructive evil.

Allows? Yes, because trauma deceives us into thinking *we dare not see good.*

I have been allowed to see several "goods" that have come from my suffering. There were the very practical "goods" that were scattered along my path—provision and help in selling my house, finding a place to stay, downsizing possessions, supporting myself—the list is long. But God cared for a multitude of such details that could have swept me under.

> *The provisions that come in the midst of suffering are good.*

Another "good" is that I know God in a depth of my being that would have otherwise remained untouched. When I originally decided that I wanted to know God, I admit I did not intend to know Him at this level. Left to myself, I would not have chosen the suffering and sacrifice that was needed to sand away the layers of who I was and reveal the raw places that would call for my utter dependence on God. I would never have gone looking for the kind of good that comes only through desperation and unimaginable pain.

Yet now I hear myself say, "I would not trade that knowledge and that awareness of God." In making that statement, do I in some peculiar way, embrace the suffering? This is a hard question to answer, because we struggle to think from an eternal perspective; it does not come naturally. But usually, as a result of suffering, our vision and our thinking begin to, in some small way, connect with the eternal mind of Christ.

Suffering can lead us to a spiritual place where we come to know God and experience His presence in a way that will change our life forever. This is good.

We learn much *about Him* in the experience of suffering. Maybe we also learn some things about ourselves.

Are you open to good in your story? Are you ready to recognize good *as God reveals it to you?*

Perhaps, you feel stuck. Maybe I can help you to begin to steer your thoughts in a positive direction by making a statement that is true: You are here! I cannot see you; but I know you are reading this. You have begun thinking and talking about your pain. You have been willing to uncover the wound and to see what it takes to clean it so that it can begin to heal. You are ready to see beauty. All of this takes courage.

Now, this is your opportunity to see good. Do not feel the need to create it. Just honestly recognize the good that was in your life, is in your life, is close to you, and is connected to you.

We will talk through this more at the approaching bend in the road, but in preparation, it might help to contemplate the following questions. As you do, remember to be truthful and to open your heart for ways to move forward through healing. Be courageous as you have this conversation with yourself.

- Are you surprised by some of the things you have done to survive? Are you surprised by some of the things you have done to make it to this day?

- Describe a few of those tasks, those mountains you climbed, those "How did I?" moments.

- Who was with you during this experience? Were there helpful hands at any point?

- Were there encouraging words? Was there uplifting music?

- What safety net of *provision* do you see, even during the darkest times?

- Is there anything you know now that you did not know before the suffering?

- What truths have come to the surface because of the pain you've endured?

By recognizing good, *you are not denying the evil.* You are simply holding the evil in its place. It is strong, but it has no right to consume you. It has no privilege to obscure the good.

Vision Therapy. *We need it.* Our eyes have been focused on one event. Consequently all information is filtered through that perspective. Like my grandson, we concentrate and show determination. However, our perspective is skewed, and we never get the results we desire. Vision Therapy might just help us train our eyes to see around and beyond and through the suffering.

It might help us to process this truth:

> *The event of our suffering is not the only subject of our story or the complete picture of our life.*

A BEND IN THE ROAD
VISION THERAPY

Let's take a deep breath and sit for some time at this bend in the road.

We have now begun to adjust our focus to include *good*. You might have found this difficult at first. I know the feeling of *sensing good but* being unable to embrace it freely and with both hands. Perhaps that is how you feel now.

This bend in the road will provide us with the "vision therapy" we need. It will gently compel our eyes and hearts to see *beyond, around,* and *through* the event, to discover the good and beauty that *are* also a part of our story.

Let's think back to the image of our life the way we tend to visualize it, in which suffering . . .

overwhelms everything,

colors all aspects of life, and

leaves very little space untouched.

Resentment. Fear. Guilt. Shame. Bitterness. Vengeful thoughts. Even a peculiar need to hold a place for pain. All nudge us to give in to the narrative of pain, allowing it to consume the picture of our lives. We feel like the suffering is touching every part of our story.

What if we were to change this image into a jigsaw puzzle, different pieces that fit together to express the story of our life? And what if we gave the suffering it's own piece?

Step back for a moment, adjust your vision, and look into your life. Focus to see ...

Positive moments

Times of provision

Blessings that kept you afloat

Current positives in your life

Look carefully. They are there. *They are always there.* Use some of the previous questions to help you bring the truth to the light. When you're ready, write three of these "goods" in the empty spaces on the puzzle.

Image # 1

Image # 2

Often, as our eyes adapt to a new perspective, more positives come into focus. As your vision adjusted to work on Image #1, perhaps more than three positives crossed your mind. Perhaps, the picture of your life expanded to include more than only that one event or emotion of suffering.

Attempt to fill in the spaces in Image #2 with more positives. You may use the previous positives from Image #1 and add more.

Do you see what happens to the event of suffering as we acknowledge more positive events, provisions, and blessings? It no longer consumes the *entire* image but begins to recede into the picture. The more blessings we add into the image, the less oppressive and consuming the trauma becomes. In a very real sense, the expression of the image, the expression of your life, becomes brighter and more clear.

This does not mean that the trauma becomes any less real. It does not mean that the effect of the trauma becomes less severe. But it does mean the trauma can become a smaller part of the overall picture—and have *less control over our everyday lives*. The *control* of the trauma can be overcome by the reality of having safety and blessings in our lives, both right now and along the way.

At the time of the crisis, the pain is so great, the fear so powerful, that we feel numb or paralyzed. It seems the event and all the emotions it brings take over every part of our lives. Trauma uses all its tactics, controlling how we respond to others, how we handle our pain, and how we express our own identity. Its script manipulates our responses, impairs our memories, and changes how we view ourselves.

We forget positive things. We forget our accomplishments. We forget our hopes. We can't process things in a healthy way. Our perspective is consumed by pain, fear, and negative memories.

The puzzle images help us see that the suffering is a very *real* part of our lives—but it is only a *part*. Throughout this journey, we have never denied the pain, as that would be unhealthy. Instead, we learned to face the reality of our suffering and its effect in our lives. Now we are simply *adding the reality* of blessings and provisions in our lives, so that we can begin to put suffering in the proper proportion.

We begin to see that there is other subject matter in our picture. There is additional scripting in our story. The suffering is receding in its pervasiveness. It exists, but it is not dominant. It happened, but it is not our identity.

We are moving forward, away from suffering, toward resolution. We are moving toward making peace with our suffering rather than feeling overwhelmed by it. Our vision therapy is helping us to adjust our focus. We are training our eyes to see accomplishments and blessings so that we can see through and around the suffering to other parts of our lives.

As we gain a new and healthy perspective, we might see that some problems become solvable. This new way of seeing might also help us to interpret and interact with the world around us in a positive and productive way.

Perhaps, we might even begin thinking about our hopes. Is it possible to see through the trauma toward the future? What do you think? Is Image #3 possible?

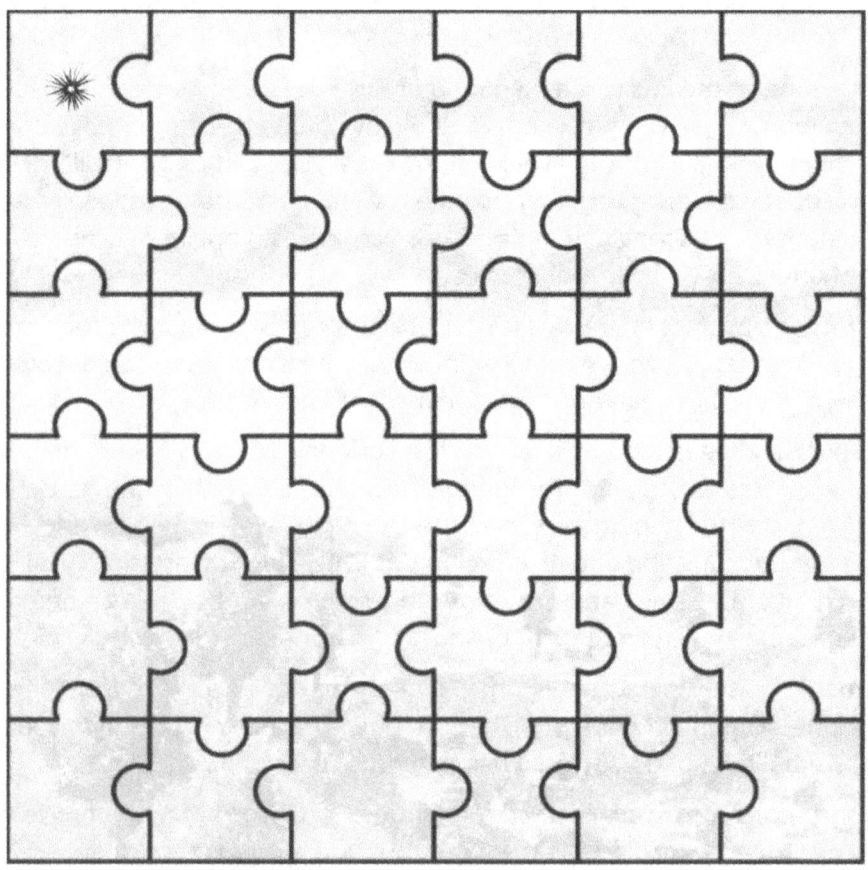

Image # 3

We are moving forward, each bend in the journey moving us along a path of healing. But what do we mean by *healing*? It's another one of those terms that carries varied expectations. So, here we should take some time to get acquainted with the word.

According to Merriam-Webster Dictionary, the definition of *heal* is "to make sound; to restore to health; to cause (an undesirable condition) to be overcome."

Ours is a contemplative journey toward *healing*. The terms *healing* and *healed* both derive from the word heal, but they carry very different connotations. *Healed* carries a meaning that suggests . . .

> the job is done.
>
> everything is good.
>
> health has been restored.
>
> the conflict has been resolved.

Healing, on the other hand, is actually the continuous verb tense of healed, which indicates that it is a continuous and indefinite process. So, as I was thinking about writing this book, I knew that I could never use the word *healed*. How arrogant it would be to leave any impression that through this journey, you would be restored to complete health. That all would be good. The job would be done.

What a heavy burden that would be for you: to be *healed*.

No, all of us—even those without devastating trauma in their story—are in the continuous process of *healing*. Not one of us has avoided the wounds and scars of this broken world. Romans 8:22-23 even says that the physical world is "groaning" as we wait eagerly for redemption. We will only be *healed* when God sets all things right in eternity. All will be good. The job will be done.

Healed is not our goal. So, as we focus on *healing*, what will that look like?

Let's consider ideas included in an *incorrect* vision of healing:

- justice is served
- there is the absence of negative feelings
- there is the absence of fear
- there are solutions to all of the practical challenges
- there is restoration or replacement of things that were lost
- others acknowledgement the wrong they inflicted on me

Sometimes, we hear people offer incorrect expectations as incentive or evidence for healing:

- "One day you will heal from this event and you won't even think about it again."
- "You just need to let yourself heal and then you won't feel those fears."
- "Healing is based on positive feelings, not on negative feelings. Let them go."

If we wait or strive to meet these types of expectations in our lives, we will continually live with the mistaken idea that we are not healing at all—and that perhaps, there is no real hope of healing.

So, what is it that we are moving towards? What is it that is beginning to happen to us through this journey? To answer those questions, we must learn to see the signals—the indications that we are moving *toward* healing, rather than huddling in place in survival mode.

The following statements provide a glimpse into some of these signals Read through them with an open mind. This is not the time to critique yourself. Simply read them as an interested bystander.

We are moving towards a place where we:
- *think beyond the next 5 minutes of survival;*
- *make plans not directly connected to the crisis;*
- *feel free to hope and anticipate good;*
- *do not carry the crisis with us as a constant companion;*
- *spend more time thinking with gratitude and less time thinking with regret;*
- *enter into the pattern of life with others.*

These are indications of one critical and profound change:

Your life's command center, the source of control, has begun to shift.

Yes, the suffering exists.

It has visited our homes, our spirits, our bodies.

But the trauma is no longer the source of control; we are no longer at its mercy.

This shift happens when the wound heals enough that other things can rub against it without causing us to flinch in pain.

It is then we find that our physical and emotional strength is no longer totally consumed by survival. Our peripheral vision of life begins to return. We begin to reconnect and interact with the humanity around us. We become ready again to feel and even express—some form of value for ourselves.

So, in past days, where we may have stood on the perimeter of everyday activities—sometimes totally unaware of other's comings and goings, other times overwhelmed by it—we are now beginning to focus on and even anticipate that movement.

Whereas before, we may have felt paralyzed by the complicated choreography of socializing, now we are stepping onto the dance floor, beginning to connect and interact—whether that's becoming aware of the people on the sidewalk waiting to cross the street, talking with the person who cuts your hair, or reconnecting with a family member.

Simple actions that once seemed overwhelming now begin to make sense—getting the appropriate rest, regaining the ability to eat (or not eat), taking care of yourself.

These are all signs of forward movement through healing.

A place where . . .

we live with an awareness of our suffering *and* our blessings.

we see our words of hope becoming reality, and

we sense our value coming to life.

WHAT ABOUT GOD?

*The idea of chaotic suffering
without God
is a hopeless plight.
However, even when we
invite God into this conversation,
we struggle to find
a comfortable place to settle.*

41
VOICING THE QUESTION

We have been walking this journey for a while now. Taking time to sit and ponder. Working on difficult challenges. Gaining strength. Even discovering peace. We can now almost see the foot path taking us forward through the suffering and toward healing.

So, it is at this very point that I feel compelled to slow down for a significant and pivotal conversation. Though it is difficult, this topic is so intertwined with our journey of healing that to ignore it any longer would be harmful to our forward movement.

In the midst of all the hard work and positive effort, there may be a question that lingers: "Why?"

- I try to do the right things. So, why did this happen?

- I try to treat others well. Why would someone hurt me in this way?

- I believe in God. Why didn't He take care of me?

- People say everything happens for a purpose. What good could come from this?

- How could God stand by and let this happen?

- Why me? Why now? Why this?

It's time that we give voice to the question: "Why?" This question often floats into our minds or words, and it is usually . . .

> shouted with accusation,
>
> murmured in restrained frustration, or
>
> whispered in silent suffering.

It's a question that longs for an answer and yet does not seem to expect one that will satisfy. In the moment of our query, we can imagine no why that could justify the incomprehensible suffering.

Those among us who choose to leave God out of all conversation often find this question a justification of that decision. "There must be no God," they say, "for what God could exist alongside such suffering?" And yet that very belief leaves them in an unsettling and solitary place, where they must create their own reasons for the whys. These reasons are limited, confusing, and unwise, and often result in more questions than answers:

- Is there a constant unseen battle of good versus evil? Does suffering exist because, for a moment, evil is more powerful? If so, is good strong enough to keep the world from eventually imploding in permanent destruction?

- Is there simply cosmic chaos, with no rhyme or reason? Is suffering part of an evolutionary process? And if so, must we just accept the unfortunate purposeless fate that comes upon us?

- Or are positive and negative in balance? If so, could it be that something I did merited suffering? Are we all just caught in the continual struggle to tip the scales in our favor?

These explanations do not feel right; nor do they prove themselves when carried out to the full extent of logic. We are left with more questions than answers.

The idea of chaotic suffering without God is a hopeless plight. However, even when we invite God into this conversation, we struggle to find a comfortable place to settle. Perhaps, we are even frustrated to have to bring this up to Him. We think, *How can I be faced with this situation when I have spoken of You with such confidence? I don't want to accuse . . . but, here I am.*

We want answers. Yet, our pain insists that there are no good ones. It's time to head into our next bend in the road.

A BEND IN THE ROAD
VOICING THE QUESTION

Over the next several chapters, we will hear more about this question and ponder some answers. Before then, however, you might want to take some time and voice your own whys in the space below.

When you express your why's, do so openly. With no filters. And with no expectation of "good" answers.

FOUR COMMON WHYS

Even with all the helpful and healing conversations we've had, one haunting question continues to surface, even when we want to set it aside: "Why did this have to happen?"

"Why suffering?" is a familiar question and debate. We will not solve it here, but we will discover some principles that can help us come to peace with the idea of suffering.

We will use four questions to help us along this part of the journey:

- Why is there suffering in the world?

- Why did suffering happen to me?

- Where is God in my suffering?

- Why did God allow this to happen?

Over the next chapters, we will look at these principles, spending a chapter on each question so that we do not rush through this part of the journey. Let's take time to ponder each one as we allow the questions and the answers to put down roots.

Before we move on, however, I must stop and clarify once again: The truths that we discover over the next few chapters will help us in our search for peace with suffering, *but they will not explain or justify the evil that has caused your pain.* The reason for this conversation is not to seek validation for the evil, injustice, or abuse. The "why" questions we will ask will not be expecting an answer that balances the scale, as that scale cannot be balanced from any human perspective. Rather, the truths we will learn about suffering are intended to help us come to peace with our suffering and, perhaps, with our Traveling Companion as well.

Ultimately, though, my hope is that the the truths we discover about suffering might calm this unsettling and disturbing distraction—the whys —that can keep us from continuing *through* our suffering, *toward* healing.

After all, that is our journey—through suffering and toward healing.

For this discussion, we return to the very beginning: the story of creation. God created a beautiful world and declared it *good*. He created humanity in His image to live in this wonderful place—and in particular, in the garden of Eden. How can we even imagine what it was like? Maybe we think mostly of the things that were *not* there. There were no weeds in the garden. There was no illness. No wars. No pain. No suffering. Adam and Eve, the first man and woman, were blessed. It was a peaceful, good, and right time.

Then, there was an event that changed everything. God gave instructions: "You are free to eat from any tree in the garden; but you must not eat from the tree of the knowledge of good and evil, for when you eat from it you will certainly die" (Genesis 2:16-17). We need to understand something very important: God always has good reason for His instructions and guidance. It is most often to protect us, to prepare us, or to provide for us. By His instruction to "not eat," God was protecting Adam and Eve from the consequences of this tree's fruit. But His reason was more far-reaching than that.

God was protecting you and me and His entire creation from the destructive consequences of the fruit of that tree—the knowledge of good *and evil*.

We won't go into all the whys and hows of this event. We will cut straight to the information that leads us to answers: Adam and Eve both ate from the one forbidden tree. They disobeyed the instructions that God had given them in order to protect them.

Disobedience brings consequences. And here is where *we* enter the story. This event was so pivotal that the consequences affected everyone and everything from that point forward, even to our lives today. At that moment, death entered the world. At that moment, illness, pain, and war entered the world. At that moment, suffering entered the world. Adam and Eve were living with the knowledge of good—and that was good—but this tree opened the door to knowing *evil*, as well.

Adam and Eve's disobedience led to devastating consequences: the knowledge of evil not only entered the world but came upon all humanity. The beautiful creation that God put into place ended up in bondage to decay and suffering (Romans 8:8-21). Taking this further, Romans 5:12 says that when the sin of disobedience entered the world, it brought death with it, and *death* now touches all people.

Now, because of that one event, *the world is broken*. There is physical illness and disease. There are wars. There are evil deeds. And there are natural disasters. We see the evidence of death in many places, from our aging process to evil that attempts to overshadow beauty, through abuse, injustice, and other destructive means.

It makes sense. We see it all around us. Why is there suffering in this world? *There is suffering because this world is broken.*

But it gets more personal than that, doesn't it? The world's brokenness becomes *our own experience*. We experience physical illness and disease. We experience war. We experience the evil deeds of others. We experience natural disasters. We experience the brokenness of this world through suffering. We experience *the knowledge of evil*.

At our next bend in the road, we'll take a moment to consider this broken world and what the knowledge of evil has meant for us all.

A BEND IN THE ROAD
WHY THERE IS SUFFERING

What evidence do you see of the world's brokenness? Take time to think about and list some of the ways that death and the knowledge of evil can be seen in the world today.

44
WHY DID SUFFERING HAPPEN TO ME?

Why me?

This world is broken—and so, suffering is here. There is no going back. We see it every day. We read about it, we hear about it, and sometimes, we are touched by it in a very personal way.

Imagine walking down a road. The road is pristine and clean. There are no potholes. There is no dust and no mud. You can walk on it freely, wearing your best shoes, and not get dirty.

Then the road begins to change. Dust begins to appear. Soon, there are potholes. At first, they are small enough that you can walk around them; by slightly changing your direction, you can avoid them and remain untouched and clean. But the holes keep getting wider and deeper. Then a car drives by, hits one of the potholes, and sprays you with muddy water. The dirt and muck of the road are now on you. The road is in such poor condition now that its effects cannot be avoided any longer.

When you arrive at your destination, others see the markings—mud splashes and dust and filthy shoes. If they were to ask, "Why are you in such a condition?" you might respond, "Because there was no way to avoid it. Mud and dust and potholes and cars were part of the road I had to travel."

The same is true for life. Pain, evil, illness and disasters are all part of it. There is no way to avoid them completely. *The brokenness and suffering are part of the road we must travel.*

This insight is helpful. Actually, it is necessary. Just like our initial awareness of suffering and loss, we must *see* that it is there before we can do anything to heal from it.

There are some who would tell you that if you just do the right thing, God will keep you from suffering. This is not true. In fact, God tells us often to *expect* suffering. Take 1 Peter 4:12, for example: "Dear friends, do not be surprised at the fiery ordeal that has come on you . . . as though something strange were happening to you." We cannot live *perfectly* enough to avoid suffering, because suffering is *in* this broken world—and so are we. Jesus lived a perfect life, and yet He experienced suffering in this world. It is part of the road that we humans travel.

Similarly, some people teach that you can avoid suffering if you just "have enough faith." I do not find this teaching anywhere in God's Word either. In fact, God records many stories to tell us that the men and women who put their faith in Him *will definitely* have suffering in their lives. In fact, it seems that the people whom God chooses for great works are often the ones who suffer the most.

For now, answering the question of why suffering happened to you and to me is quite straightforward:

We experience suffering because we live in this world.

We experience suffering because it is part of the road we must travel.

Wait, no! you might be thinking. That answer does not seem personal enough. I'm just on the muddy road with everyone else? There must be more to the story.

The next conversation we have will be more personal. For now, it is crucial that we understand this basic truth of common suffering or we will go back to "Why, me?" over and over again. We cannot heal from our suffering or face future suffering in a healthy way, if we do not grasp this truth:

The world is broken.

We now have knowledge of good *and* evil.

We are going to be touched by suffering simply because we are here.

Let's stop for a bend in the road.

A BEND IN THE ROAD

WHY SUFFERING HAPPENED TO US

What personal experience do you have of the world's brokenness? How have you been touched by suffering? What knowledge of evil do you now have that you did not seek? What splashes of mud and grime have left marks on you, your family or those you love? Take some time to acknowledge the brokenness that has touched your life.

45
WHERE IS GOD IN THE SUFFERING?

So far, we've learned that there is suffering because this world is broken, and we experience suffering because we live in this world. But if suffering is in this world and I must experience it, *then where is God in the suffering?*

You have gathered by now that God is my closest traveling companion and the one I completely trust. I include Him in all conversations along my journey. Perhaps, He is a close companion of yours as well. Or, perhaps, you regard Him as a distant, uninvolved acquaintance. Or maybe He is still unfamiliar, even unwelcome. There is no pressure here. I only ask that you remain open to the conversation—the possibilities—as we move forward.

We often try to define what God does and what He intends. And we often base our definitions of God on cultural or religious traditions, changing philosophies, our own desires and fears. However, when we consider who God is, it would be wise to consider what *He says about Himself.* After all, who God is lays the foundation upon which all our conclusions must stand —about suffering and about life in general. Perhaps it is more correct to say that "what we choose to believe about God" lays the foundation for our conclusions. A person who chooses to believe that there is no God or that He is not involved in our lives will approach life much differently that a person who sees God as a trustworthy companion and guide. Let's see what He has to say about Himself.

God describes Himself in multiple ways—too many for this book! So, we will look at just four aspects of who He is, which will help with our discussion over the chapters that follow. The first three, which we will cover here, are about God being "all" in some area.

1. God is ALL-KNOWING OR OMNISCIENT

> Do you not know? Have you not heard? The LORD is the everlasting God, the Creator of the ends of the earth. He will not grow tired or weary, and his understanding no one can fathom. (Isaiah 40:28)

> Nothing in all creation is hidden from God's sight. Everything is uncovered and laid bare to the eyes of him to whom we must give account. (Hebrews 4:13)

> Before a word is on my tongue, you, LORD, know it completely. (Psalm 139:4)

God knows ALL. Nothing takes place outside of His knowledge. This includes the suffering in your life. No one can do anything to you that God does not know about. So, we cannot say, "God did not know this could or would happen."

2. God is ALL-PRESENT, OR OMNIPRESENT.

> "Am I only a God nearby," declares the LORD, "and not a God far away? Who can hide in secret places so that I cannot see them?" declares the LORD. "Do not I fill heaven and earth?" (Jeremiah 23:23-24)

> Where can I go from Your Spirit? Where can I flee from Your presence? . . . If I rise on the wings of the dawn, if I settle on the far side of the sea, even there your hand will guide me, your right hand will hold me fast. If I say, "Surely the darkness will hide me and the light become night around me," even the darkness will not be dark to you; the night will shine like the day, for darkness is as light to you. (Psalm 139:7, 9-12)

God is present EVERYWHERE. There is no tiny corner where God cannot be. Therefore, God is present in our suffering. He is not hiding or preoccupied. We cannot say, "God was not present when the suffering happened."

3. God is ALL-POWERFUL OR OMNIPOTENT.

"I am the LORD, the God of all mankind. Is there anything too hard for me?" (Jeremiah 32:27)

All the peoples of the earth are regarded as nothing. He does what he pleases with the powers of heaven and the peoples of the earth. No one can hold back his hand or say to him, "What have you done?" [Daniel 4:35]

ALL power belongs to God. He displays it every day for those who are willing to see. The person who harmed you does not have more power than God. Even all of nature bows to His power and authority. So, we can be sure that God has the power to confront all instruments of suffering. We cannot say: "God was powerless against my suffering."

All-knowing. All-present. All-powerful. Let's stop for a moment before we visit the fourth aspect of who He is and see how these first three characteristics of God help our conversation.

Where is God in the suffering? He is not ignorant, unaware, or distracted. He is not far off. He is not powerless, with His hands tied. The truth brings this conclusion:

God is present with us in our suffering.

No! Perhaps, your heart is shouting or whispering . . . *No.*

Somehow, we feel comfortable including God in the conversation of *healing,* but we often recoil when an attempt is made to include Him in the actual event—in *the experience of suffering.*

We don't want Him in that place of confusion. There is a risk of feeling anger or bitterness toward Him. There is the danger of feeling He's betrayed us. We don't know what to do with Him, standing there in the presence of evil and pain.

But please stay with me. We must follow the path honestly if we are to make sense of this conversation and discover truth that can hold up under the devastating pressure of suffering and the desperate need to come to peace with it. We cannot cling to nice assurances that do not follow through to logical conclusions. If we are to come to peace with suffering—and include

God in that conversation—then the answers must make sense. We are taking our time with this part of the journey because you might feel the same.

That said, in our attempt to keep God outside the actual image of suffering, we often create our own theories that attempt to explain away the whys of suffering in our lives:

Theory 1:

The brokenness of the world has led to chaotic events. (Think back on the potholes in the road.) So, there are times when my life gets caught in the chaos, and random things happen. It is a bit like being in the wrong place at the wrong time. The suffering I experience is at the whim of the chaos.

Truth:

It certainly appears that the world is in chaos. However, even the apparent chaos is under the authority of God's hand. Think back to what we know to be true about God. He is all-knowing, all-present, and all-powerful. If chaos rules, then God is not God. If God is God, then the chaos has boundaries.

There is a brilliant description of the intricacies of God's power, knowledge, and authority in Job 38-41. It's a good read. It makes me smile, cry, and laugh, and it always reassures me of who is holding the boundaries in this crazy world as I see so many run onto the stage and claim authority and power.

> Where were you when I laid the earth's foundation? Who marked off its dimensions? (Job 38:4-5)
>
> Have you ever given orders to the morning, or shown the dawn its place? (Job 38:12)
>
> Does the eagle soar at your command and build its nest on high? (Job 39:27)

Other places in God's Word also assure us that the events of our life are not left to chaos; they are not random. Consider this passage in Psalm 139:16: "[His] eyes saw [your] unformed body; all the days ordained for [you] were written in [His} book before one of them came to be." [Psalm 139:16].

Theory 2:

God gives humankind free will. God allows people to choose whether to do right or wrong, or even whether to do evil. My pain is only the result of another person's free will used unwisely.

Truth:

The term "free will" is vague and often misused. Free? Well, not exactly. The choices we make are limited by our physical and mental capabilities, among other things. It is more accurate to say that God gives us the privilege and accountability of decision-making, in that He does not treat us as puppets or manipulate us.

Although God gives us the privilege of choice, however, He is not at the mercy of the will of man. In a moment, we might find ourselves unable to overpower or refuse the actions of someone due to a differential in age, strength or authority. We might even feel that we are at the mercy of a physical disease or other circumstances. Yet, ulitmately, in light of the descriptive of God—all-knowing, all-present all-powerful—this truth remains: everything that happens in my life has passed through my Father's "ALL" hands. This is true even when I feel at the mercy of another person or influence.

Let's go back to Job for a moment. The evil one had to go to God and request permission to inflict suffering on Job (see Job 1-2). God had to set—and remove—the boundaries. The same is true in our lives. God does not create evil (remember, we learned how it entered the world in the previous chapter), but evil *does* submit to Him and cannot step over His boundaries.

I assure you that you are not at the mercy of man's will. God shows us this in His Word:

> So do not fear, for I am with you; do not be dismayed, for I am your God. I will strengthen you and help you; I will uphold you with my righteous right hand. (Isaiah 41:10)

> Are not two sparrows sold for a penny? Yet not one of them will fall to the ground outside your Father's care. And even the very hairs of your head are all numbered. So don't be afraid; you are worth more than many sparrows. (Matthew 10:29-31).

Where does this leave us in our why questions?

> There is suffering in the world because it broken.

> We experience suffering because we live in this world.

> God, being all-knowing, all-present, all-powerful, is with us in our suffering.

>> We are not at the mercy of chaos.

>> We are not at the mercy of man's will.

>> *God is with me in my suffering.*

This is such an amazing mystery. Beautiful. Profound. Mind-stretching.

I love the word *mystery.* It has become a bigger part of my spiritual journey over time. Now is the time to share it with you. The spiritual mysteries that we encounter are not the kind that can be solved by gathering clues. Spiritual mysteries are those concepts that are beyond our understanding. These mysteries are the indescribable, incomprehensible, and wonderful aspects of God that we simply embrace. Sometimes, we have to say, "I can't explain it."

Our conversation about God's involvement in our suffering must include *mystery.*

God's desire is that I embrace His presence in my journey—all of it. His desire is also that I embrace His presence in my suffering, because only then can I accept that there is purpose in my suffering. We have more to consider about that—but first, a bend in the road.

A BEND IN THE ROAD

WHERE GOD IS
IN THE SUFFERING

In what ways have I reasoned away my suffering to the general chaos of the world?

In what ways have I reasoned away my suffering to the will of others?

How can I open my heart and my mind to the presence of God in my suffering?

46

WHY DID GOD ALLOW THIS TO HAPPEN?

Even as we ponder the truth that *God is present with us in our suffering,* there follows another *"why?"*

If God knows about our suffering, is with us in our suffering, and is more powerful than our suffering, then, *why oh why did He not stop it? Why did He not intervene?*

This is the perfect time to hear about the fourth characteristic of this One who is on the journey with us.

4. *He is GOOD.*

> Praise the LORD, for the LORD is good. (Psalm 135:3)

> You are good, and what you do is good. (Psalm 119:68)

God wants us to come to a place where we accept His goodness personally. This can be hard, because His goodness to us does not always *feel* good.

Some say God is not good because He allows little children to go hungry. Some say God is not good because He allows floods and storms and wars and illness and sorrow of all kinds. Maybe you feel that God is not good because He did not stop the suffering that came into your life.

Remember that He knows all, including our questions and doubts. Listen to what He tells us:

> "For my thoughts are not your thoughts, neither are your ways my ways," declares the LORD. "As the heavens are higher than the earth, so are my ways higher than your ways and my thoughts than your thoughts." (Isaiah 55:8-9)

This does not mean that He thinks little of our pain. In fact, God feels the pain to a greater extent than even we can; He sees layer upon layer of circumstances and events. His heart always turns toward the oppressed, the weak, the suffering.

Rather, God is telling us that there is so much more to our story than even we know, that He knows beyond what we can know, and that He is always participating in our lives with a purpose that is eternal.

Remember Joseph's story, recorded in Genesis 37-50? He was mocked and slandered by his brothers who, after deciding not to murder him, sold him into captivity in a faraway land. Things got better for a time, but then he was falsely accused and imprisoned, where he was forgotten and set aside. Eventually, he came to a place of authority in the land, and God used him to save many lives. Years later, when he reunited with the brothers, his response to them and all the suffering he endured was interesting: "You intended to harm me, but God intended it for good to accomplish what is now being done, the saving of many lives" (Genesis 50:20).

Do you recognize the four characteristics of our Traveling Companion?

God *saw* Joseph's suffering (He is omniscient); God was present with Joseph in his suffering (He is omnipresent); and God had power over those who caused Joseph's suffering (He is omnipotent). God, in His goodness (He is good), also had an intention—a purpose—for Joseph's suffering. God was "ALL" in the events of Joseph's life.

This brings us to a pivotal point in our perspective of suffering:

> *You can know with certainty that God is ALL in your life*
> *in such a way that He will not allow the actions of others*
> *to change His plan for you.*

No one is more powerful than God. No one can sneak in and change God's plan for you while He is not looking. No one can fight Him for control of your life and win. Even though people may make decisions that impact your life in some way, it is always *within God's knowledge, His sight,* and *His power— within His boundaries.*

How do we respond when that is difficult—the circumstances seem unjust, unfair? We must embrace the perfect goodness of God.

Your suffering has purpose.

A BEND IN THE ROAD

MY RESPONSE TO THE POSSIBILITY OF GOOD

How do I respond to the idea of "good" when it doesn't look good or feel good?

How would it impact my everyday life and my potential for healing if I could trust that there is one person who truly only wants my good and has the power to back it up?

47

A VISUAL OF SUFFERING

You have been patient over the last few chapters as we have delved into the depths of pain and our response to it. Yet, I am aware that, as much as I can agonize over the necessary words to bring this discussion to life, and as much as you can read it with openness and determination, our minds and hearts will each interpret the conversation based on our own life perspectives. As such, this seems to be an important moment to turn to visual expression.

I ask you to set your crisis aside for a moment. Now, let's just walk together through this visual expression of suffering in our lives. These images might bring our expectations—as well as reality—to life.

Let's begin with our expectations. Many of us tend to anticipate life's journey to look like this:

Green grass, blue sky.

A few clouds, but nothing too overwhelming.

Shade available as needed.

And when there is no immediate crisis,

we can typically maintain this image of life.

But then . . . moments of crisis—followed by suffering—enter the picture.

We desperately respond by attempting to put the former image back into place, so that we can move on with life as it *should* be.

How do we explain the appearance of such unwelcome disruptions?

If we follow our previous conclusion that God has accountability in those events, we are likely a bit perturbed.

How could He allow those moments to disturb a previously beautiful image? we think. Why would He do that? Is He uncaring or even cruel? Is He unaware? Is He weak against evil? I thought He loved us and was looking out for us!

The problem is that our image is skewed. We have been building the foundation of our reasoning on an incorrect visual.

You see, as related to suffering, this is the true image of our journey in this world:

The road is muddy and full of potholes.

Moments of crisis are all around us.

Opportunities for suffering abound.

Evil is active, seeking ways to undo us.

Most of these realities are unseen, unfelt, and unrecognized.

But, the truth is *they are there.*

So, the reality is not that our lives look like green grass and blue sky until God, unthinkingly and without reason, allows moments of crisis to enter.

The reality is that we are surrounded by moments of crisis from the very beginning—because the world is broken and has been opened to the knowledge and influence of evil. And we are living in the midst of it.

This picture of reality can feel discouraging or even distressing. But by gaining more insight into the image, we can see the situation more accurately. Look carefully, and you can see that there is someone present who is very important in this conversation.

Here He is—our companion on the journey.

Ruler of ALL:
Who sees all.
Who knows all.
Who is all powerful.

This Ruler of ALL
sees every potential
suffering that is part of
the brokenness
of our world.

As that brokenness becomes more personal, He becomes more involved in your life—mitigating, protecting, being attentive to every crisis that either hovers around you or threatens from afar.

In His perfect knowledge of you, and in His profound awareness of good, He allows only particular moments of crisis to touch your life. When one crisis touches your life, there are many others from which He protects you.

The suffering that touches you does not do so at the whim of chaos or at the will of others; it is filtered through His loving hands. And so, there is more to the picture.

Meet Christ, The Good Shepherd.

Whenever the Ruler of All filters suffering through His all-knowing hands and allows it to touch your life in a personal way, the Good Shepherd steps into that moment with you.

What does that mean for us?

It means that He increases our strength, both physical and emotional, beyond what we think we have. Perhaps you have said this as I have: "How did I do that? How did I make it through?"

Our Good Shepherd added His strength so that we could accomplish the tasks, large and small, that were beyond our meager capabilities.

- It means that He encourages us, sometimes through other people and sometimes through our awareness of His presence.

- It means that He gives discernment when we do not know what decision to make.

- It means that, whether He is walking alongside you or carrying you, at every moment, His eyes are on you and His heart is for you.

These images speak clearly: The world is broken. Suffering and evil abound. But you are not at the mercy of chaos, random events, or the evil intent of others. Rather, God protects you from much suffering. God filters what will be allowed to touch your life. God stands in the suffering with you and draws the boundaries that determine to what extent it can touch you.

What truth becomes clear to us?

> There is no suffering where God is not present.
>
> With God, there is no suffering without purpose.
>
> With God, there is no suffering that can destroy us.
>
> With God, there is always the potential for healing.

These may be truths that we know about God—in our minds. But these truths will not impact our healing until we embrace them into our emotions and our heart. It might not happen all at once—one great decision. Our Traveling Companion is patient, remaining close with persistent words of assurance.

There are times when past events of my life sweep over me, one after another, and I remember the devastating effects. I lift my gaze to the heavens and whisper, "Was that really necessary?"

The simple answer comes: *"I am* ALL. *I am* GOOD. *There has been purpose in your suffering."*

If we are to move forward through healing, how do we do so with sure footing? We can choose to embrace and give ourselves to . . .

> the whim of chaos,
>
> the will of others,
>
> OR
>
> the hands of a God who is ALL and GOOD.

I have found unspeakable surety, courage, strength, and peace by including God in my journey of healing. Are there unanswered questions? Does it include mystery? Yes. But, should I not expect that from a God who is truly God?

A BEND IN THE ROAD
TIME TO PONDER

We need some time to think, to ponder. Breathe deeply.

Then think about these truths:

God *was* with you in your suffering.

God *is* with you today.

God *will be* with you in the future, whatever comes.

Use this space to express your emotions.

We were introduced to Naomi very early on in our journey. Naomi moved away from her home, family, and culture into a strange land. She lost her husband, and, then as a widow, she faced the loss of her two sons.

We are returning to Naomi's story because, in her journey of suffering, she lived out this very awareness of God that we have been discussing.

Naomi might have given in to the numbness and despair, but *she did not*. She did not have every answer; she did not know what new challenges awaited her. She just kept listening to the quiet voice inside that called her forward— out of the numbness. She took steps to move forward in and through her pain and away from her pain. And in that process, *Naomi told her story.*

As we listen in on that story, we learn much about Naomi and God. Remember, she didn't wrap up her pain in a pretty package and pretend to have answers for it. Rather, she told her story of sadness and loss with honest emotion and truthful words. She opened her heart and let it spill forth:

> "Don't call me Naomi," she told them. "Call me Mara, because the Almighty has made my life very bitter. I went away full, but the LORD has brought me back empty. Why call me Naomi? The LORD has afflicted me; the Almighty has brought misfortune upon me." (Ruth 1:20–21)

Naomi spoke the raw truth of the situation while *also* expressing her understanding of God. As she expressed her suffering, God became a natural part of that expression.

Essentially, she was saying,

"My loss leaves me feeling empty."

"The events of my life taste bitter to me. I feel afflicted, burdened."

"I remember how I used to feel, and now the blessing is gone. And it all happened by the hand of God."

In response to this passage, there are those who say that Naomi *blamed* God; but it is more accurate to say that Naomi *placed the responsibility* for the suffering on God. There is a subtle but important difference. Blame is often cast upon someone with an accusation of unfairness or neglect. Naomi, however, spoke of God with the highest and most profound worship, while at the same time acknowledging her pain through His hand.

To this point, notice what Naomi did *not* say:

"Why has God allowed this to happen to me? I don't deserve this suffering."

"God is not fair."

"I will no longer trust God because of this suffering."

"This suffering proves to me that there is no God."

Naomi did not blame God. She recognized that her pain was not due to chaotic events or the result of her—or others'—wrong choices. Rather, Naomi's words reveal that she saw her suffering clearly—and, even more importantly, that she saw God's hand in it!

Seeing that God was in her suffering did not frighten her. In fact, understanding that her affliction had passed through her Father's hands is what gave her the confidence to launch out again into the unknown. Her awareness of God in her suffering is what kept her in conversation with Him. And it is that awareness that made it possible for her to hear His voice, saying, "Move forward."

> Naomi felt suffering to the depth of her being.
> But she knew to that same depth that God was there.
> God. The Almighty. The LORD. Her LORD.

Likewise, the conversation we have with God during suffering is extremely important. God is aware when we are simply saying what we think He wants us to say or what others dictate to us. But it is our honest conversation with Him that will eventually lead us to a place where we can make peace with the suffering and peace with God.

49
WHERE IS GOD IN THE STORM?

Did God know?   Did He allow?
Is it part of His plan for me?

As I consider all the truths about my God and thoughtfully apply them to my life,
I come to a compelling conclusion.

My God is aware of the storm of suffering on the horizon.
He sees. He knows.

My God is powerful enough to prevent it or steer me in another direction.
And often, He does.

There are other times, however, that He takes my hand and,
full of loving intention, says,

"Come, child. We are going to walk into that storm.

I am coming with you, and I will not leave your side.

I will cover you with my feathers of protection,

and under my wings you will take refuge.

I will whisper 'to the right' or 'to the left.'

Trust my purpose for you.   Trust my goodness.

Trust my love for you.

Trust me."

Oh dearest Father,

"You hem me in behind and before and you lay your hand upon me. Such
knowledge is too wonderful for me, too lofty for me to attain . . . All the days
ordained for me were written in your book before one of them came to be.
How precious to me are your thoughts, O God!" Psalm 139:5

GOD IS WITH ME IN MY SUFFERING.

This is not my fear; this is my unshakeable assurance.

50

SEEING SUFFERING IN A NEW WAY

So far on this journey, our focus has been on the experience of our suffering and, in particular, the negative effects of our suffering. However, I have hesitated to call suffering bad or to label it as evil—because as much as we try to run from it and protect ourselves from it, *suffering is not the bad guy*.

Do I feel some pushback? You may be saying, "Suffering is the root of my problem. If not for the suffering, I would be doing just fine!"

Consider these possibilities:

Suffering is a means for us to grow in courage and strength.

Suffering reveals truths about ourselves.

Suffering encourages us to ponder what we believe;
without it, we rarely stop at the bends in the road.

Suffering connects us to others.

Suffering connects us to Jesus, as He also suffered on this earth.

Suffering is a powerful way to express the reality of God's presence in our lives.

We know that suffering is natural, expected, unavoidable. But what if we consider that suffering is also *good*—a blessing even, as well as a necessary ingredient in our lives if we are to grow in courage, strength, and peace?

What if suffering is the distinctive thread in our tapestry that defines and reflects all of the other colors in order to display life's true beauty?

A BEND IN THE ROAD
SEEING SUFFERING
IN A NEW WAY

Consider the possibilities of suffering outlined on the previous page. Below, add thoughts about your new relationship with suffering. The potential is there. Dig deep. Open your heart to this new relationship.

HOPE

*Our desire for hope reaches out and
lands often on wishful thinking.
Rather than compromising our
expectations, rather than entrusting
ourselves to one undependable wish
after another, we long for
a source of true hope.*

What is hope? What have you heard about it? What do you think it is?

Sometimes it seems hope is offered as a vague antidote to suffering, leading to more questions than answers.

> "Just have hope!" people say.
>> *Is it a magic medicine that cures all ills?*
>
> Or, "If all else fails—hope!"
>> *Is it a last resort?*
>
> "If you only have enough hope . . . "
>> *Is it something measured by quantity?*

We often pretend that we know what we (and others) mean by *hope*. We figure it must be a good thing to talk about during hard times. And so, we smile and agree and say, "Yes, I have *hope*. Isn't it wonderful?"

Yet deep down inside, we are not sure. Often, *despair* seems more realistic than *hope*. Despair says that our choices do not matter because nothing will ever change. Despair says that the bad always wins. Despair is the absence of hope.

On the news, in our lives, the evidence seems to stack up on the side of despair. Sometimes, we can physically *feel* its presence. It presses in upon us, threatening to smother. In its oppressiveness, it seems to challenge us to push back. It hovers over us as we consider the potential outcomes of our decisions, making it difficult to think clearly.

And yet, as strongly as despair presents its case, something innate in human nature prompts us to reach toward something else—and hope seems like the right thing. This is why we see so many sayings about hope —on garden stones, on artwork, on posters, on bumper stickers.

Things like,

> Don't lose hope. You never know what tomorrow may bring.
>
> Hope is the little voice you hear whisper "Maybe" when the entire world is shouting "Not possible!"
>
> With hope, anything is possible.
>
> Embrace hope and tomorrow will be better.

What? Perhaps you respond as I do to these sugary expressions of uselessness. The words leave us with the feeling of "maybe" rather than the conviction of real hope. They make it seem as if hope is an unlikely outcome that we try to conjure up just to keep ourselves from jumping off a cliff!

So, let's try to gain some clarity.

First, we need a correct understanding of the term *hope*. There are two clearly defined and legitimate definitions of hope. We will consider the first definition in this chapter.

Culturally and secularly, hope usually carries a feeling of expectation and a desire for a particular thing, *usually a good thing*, to happen. Examples include,

> I *hope* you feel better.
>
> I *hope* it doesn't rain today.
>
> I *hope* I get that job.
>
> I *hope* I can pay my bills.

Expressed this way, hope is the expression of *a* desire for something good to happen. It expresses the very real *possibility* of good and the determination to take a chance on that possibility. It suggests an ability to look forward with longing, if not confidence. And it opens the door to something other than despair. This is good. We need this perspective.

Yet, packed within this use of the word *hope* is the understanding that the outcome is uncertain. If we were sure of the outcome, we would not use the word hope. Instead, we would say, "I *know* you will feel better," "I *have been assured of* a job offer," or "I *will* have the money to pay my bills."

We often use *hope* as an expression of what we want to happen, or what we wish will happen; yet choosing to use the word *hope* rather than the word know *is* to acknowledge the *possibility of disappointment.* Deep in our hearts, we know there is a chance that what we want *may not actually come to be.*

Isn't that interesting? The very word that is used to express possibility is packaged with the potential for failure. In that sense, *hope* takes on a sad tone, doesn't it? We can sometimes even hear this in the tone of voice with which hopefulness is spoken: "Well, I *hope* that works out."

One of the results of the suffering in our lives is that we often feel trapped, as if we are in an oppressive and threatening place and don't know how to find our way out. Our thoughts of the future are overshadowed by the pain of the past and the present. So, how can we have hope for something good when all is tainted by pain?

Sometimes the pain seems so great that we can't see any hope that it will get better. Sometimes, if our trauma involves harm that was done to someone else, we might even feel guilty about having hope. We might think, *Why should something good happen to me when others were harmed so deeply?* And especially if our suffering is ongoing, we might not see any hope of moving beyond the current status quo.

These feelings are all very natural and real. Deep inside, we feel nothing can change. We are convinced that "life the way it is" is "life the way it will always be." In the midst of our suffering, we become unwilling to take a chance on good. We do not—cannot—choose to *hope,* because we are overwhelmed by the surety of failure and the surety of pain. To live this way is to *live in* despair.

So, here we sit, either . . .

> hoping—expectantly wishing, without any real assurance for good,
> OR
> giving into despair, because we see no possibility that good will overcome suffering.

In the next chapter, we will talk about a more assured sense of hope. But, for now, as difficult as it may be, we are going to stop for a bend in the road.

A BEND IN THE ROAD

GIVING VOICE
TO MY HOPES

Set aside contemplative time to express your thoughts and emotions about hope.

Your hopes are valuable. We record valuable things. Use this page to express your hopes. Truthfully with words and phrases, identify those things *for which you had hoped,* as well as those things for which you still hope. Be a good traveling companion—do not respond, "Well, I never should have hoped for that." You should have hoped. You did hope. Let's acknowledge it together.

Then, perhaps more difficult, record how those hopes have been unfulfilled, crushed, or shattered. This is the time to say it. No sugary quotes. No defenses of others.

Simply and honestly hear your hopes. Give value to them *and* to the pain you have experienced.

The previous conversation left us wanting, for its definition of hope turned out to be mere wishful thinking. It offered no surety, no rescue from despair. So, is there more?

Yes, there is more. We have another definition of hope.

Used in a spiritual context, *hope* carries a far different meaning. Hope, from the spiritual perspective, is a *sure thing,* or a reliable truth or event.

Carrying this meaning, h*ope* becomes more of a noun than a verb. Let's talk about that.

Think carefully. Is there anyone or anything in your life on whom you can place your hope with *all confidence*? Some of you are starting to reply in the affirmative, but think carefully. We are not talking about "wishing" or "thinking well of" or "expecting the best of" someone or something. Considering that, it is very unlikely that there is anyone in your life who has always been or will always be a *sure hope.* And for those who come close, they can—literally—be gone in a heartbeat. In fact, one of the reasons we are working through this journey of suffering is because we had *hoped* in something or someone, only to discover that the object of our hope could not uphold our confidence—whether because of intentional betrayal on their part or simply the reality of life.

So, we can wish all we want, but there is no real possibility of something or someone being absolute and unchanging; there is no sure thing, no real hope.

Where does this leave us?

Since the object of our hope is not dependable, we shift our focus to the *act of hoping.* We hold on to *hope as a verb.* Our lives then become consumed by wishful thinking—sweet poster-sayings that fill our walls and car bumpers and even our minds. These things might calm our spirits for a time and temporarily push aside the hovering cloud of impending reality, but eventually, the variables stack up against us, and things often do not turn out "as we hope."

So, surety does not lie *in how strongly we hope* (verb); rather, it must lie in *the object of our hope* (noun). Ahhh . . . now we are getting somewhere.

To meet the requirement of being a sure thing, the object of our hope must be

unchanging,
absolutely truthful,
just,
and have perfect love.

Sounds impossible, right?

It is virtually impossible, and that is why we have learned to make concessions and excuses. The result is that we jump from one hopeful phrase to another, one wishful promise to the next. If our life journey was being watched from behind, it would appear haphazard and erratic, as we swerve from one flawed promise to another . . . and another . . . and another. It is also why we have lost our hope. Along the way, every other thing, every other person has fallen short. We know this deep inside. It is the very nature of our world.

And here is where I am asking you to listen with an open mind—or at least stay in the conversation. In the midst of the unknowns, the disappointments, and the uncertainties, there is one answer for the longing we all have for an absolute hope, for a sure thing.

Do you remember the Traveling Companion that I encouraged you to invite on this journey? It was for this very moment that I did so. Because He is

unchanging and unchangeable,
absolutely truthful,
just,
and has perfect love.

He is your Creator, and He literally holds all things together. His name is I Am.

Yes, you most often hear Him simply called God. But when *He* introduces Himself to people, He uses a variety of names, usually one that fits the moment perfectly. In the book of Exodus, when He is about to rescue His people who are *suffering* and have *lost their hope*, He calls Himself I AM.

In that story, God sends Moses as the earthly leader for His people's rescue, and Moses is unsure about asking the people to put their hope in what he has to say. He knows that they have been abused and feel that no one hears their cries for help. And now, he will ask them to put their hope in someone—and to follow through with actions to prove that hope. So, Moses asks God, "When they ask who has sent me with this hope; when they ask your name, what should I say?"

And God replies, *"Tell them I AM has sent you."*

I AM.

Similarly, I chose the I AM name for God for this chapter because it fits the moment. After honest contemplation, we have come to one conclusion:

There is no one who is worthy of our complete trust.

There is no sure thing to which we can attach our hope.

There is no one!

And our Traveling Companion says, *"I Am."*

"I AM"—a name so full of meaning and value. It holds layer upon layer of truth. As God says "I Am" He expresses His presence in the past, the present, and the future—His presence in *your* past, present, and future. God's statement of "I Am" also answers our search for someone who is trustworthy. *"I Am worthy of your complete trust. I Am dependable enough to hold your hope as a sure thing. I Am the One."*

There are some who say that God is just another poster-saying or that it is difficult to trust God because He is just a higher version of everyone else who has disappointed us. Others speak confidently about living a life with "no absolutes." There is freedom, they say, in flexibility and openness to all truths.

The reality is that when we commit to a belief system with no certainties, we commit to a belief system with no real hope. My intent for this discussion, however, is not to present a defense for the existence or nature of God. I am only saying that I cannot have a conversation about hope without introducing you to the only one who can *be* that hope.

Our Creator knows us and our need for hope, or He wouldn't have inspired this writing: "Let us *hold unswervingly* to the hope we profess, for he who promised is faithful" (Hebrews 10:23; emphasis mine).

Rather than compromising our expectations, rather than entrusting ourselves to one undependable wish after another, after another, we are to hold *unswervingly*—to what?—to *the hope Himself.* The surety comes *not in our action of hope* but in the *object of our hope:* we must "hold unswervingly to the hope . . . for he . . . is faithful."

We can *hope* (verb) for someone to be faithful, but that will not hold us in the storm. There is only One who can *be our hope* (noun). Only He can say, "*I Am*" and prove that He Is.

I know. I have held unswervingly in the storm.

We have all experienced it: The storm rages. Chaos spins around us. Our hopes are betrayed. We acknowledge the truth: If life is only a chaotic free-for-all, *there is no hope.*

But when our companion speaks—"I Am!"—our longing for hope reaches out. And we discover there is One to whom we can hold *without reservation.*

53

THE BEAUTY OF HOPE THAT DOES NOT DISAPPOINT

Yes, my soul finds rest in God; my hope comes from him. (Psalm 62:5)

God did this so that . . . we who have fled to take hold of the hope
set before us may be greatly encouraged.
We have this hope as an anchor for the soul
for the soul, firm and secure. (Hebrews 6:18-19)

But those who hope in the LORD will renew their
strength. They will soar on wings like eagles;
they will run and not grow weary,
they will walk and not be faint. (Isaiah 40:31)

May the God of hope
fill you with all joy and peace
as you trust in him, so that you may
overflow with hope . . . (Romans 15:13)

And hope does not put us to shame. (Romans 5:5)

OUR RESPONSE TO OTHERS

Our healing journey is influenced by our response to others in our story: those who experienced our pain and those who caused our pain.

54
OTHERS IN MY STORY

Thus far, we have talked about our own perspective of suffering. But there are likely other perspectives for us to consider—viewpoints of other people who have come in and out of our story of suffering. Some of these people have been good to us; others have caused us harm. Some, we will never see again, and others are still a part of our everyday lives.

The relationships in our lives can change as a result of suffering. Some bonds are broken because of actions, events, and circumstances, while others grow stronger through suffering. The change in some relationships might not be good or bad; it is just *change*. Maybe we don't understand why things are not as they once were; we only know that something is different.

All of this is okay. We have learned that new and different can be a safe place, especially because the Good Shepherd is in that new and different place with us. We have also learned that it is important to face the reality of the effects of our suffering. We know that if we ignore the changes and expect everything to stay the same as before, we will have trouble and disappointments. And so, we must think about the changes in our relationships. We must also think about our responses to those changes.

Let's begin here: each person's journey through suffering is unique.

Two people may experience the "same" event, but their journey through healing will be very different. Even though the same event touched both lives, the resulting trauma is personal to each person. The painful event affects each person's story in a way that is particular to her or him.

Think of each person taking her suffering out of the box and beginning the process toward "the way life is now." That is a very personal journey. Even if two people live in the same house or belong to the same family, each must walk a personal road of suffering and healing. Each person will have his or her own fear, hurt, anger, bitterness, and doubt.

Consider siblings or neighbors or coworkers who are trying to heal from a shared crisis. One responds in anger, while another feels great fear and guilt. A third person might not even be ready to take the suffering out of the box, pretending that all is fine. Each person is at a different place in the journey of suffering. Each one is experiencing different emotions. And as time goes on, they may even "exchange" places and swap emotions!

And then there is the timing of it all. Although several people may have been impacted by a singular event, each will need to go through his or her own timeline of healing. Family and friends who have lost a mutual loved one, for instance, mourn and face the loss on different timelines and with different intensities. One person may be on the road to healing, while another is still attempting to accept the event as reality.

Even the losses we feel will be different. There are types of loss that one person might feel very deeply and another does not. Suffering is not *compare-able*. Our suffering is personal to each of us—in its impact, in the fallout that comes after, in the ways it pushes against our everyday lives.

Because of this truth, I cannot become angry with others because they *do not share my feelings even though we shared the same experience.* I cannot force someone to feel "my" anger or share my perspective. This can be very difficult because it seems so clear to me. I feel, *This is the correct response!* But if I cause someone to feel guilty or ashamed because of her response to suffering, then I am adding to her suffering.

Perhaps, you discover a new truth—even one from this book—that helps you move forward, but when you share it with someone close to you, there is not the response you expected. There is not the relief from them that you felt for yourself. This is because you encountered that truth on your own bend in the road. It is personal to *you*.

And so, we must give each person the freedom to take his or her own journey through suffering. It will not be possible to "fix" or explain all the emotions that each person experiences along the way. Perhaps, I can share or even show my perspectives by my actions. But I cannot insist or impose my own steps forward in healing.

Suffering often involves a tangled web of details, emotions, and responses that is impossible to lay out in a way that all involved will be satisfied. It might help to think about the way we interpret and express our pain as a complicated puzzle. Often, we don't even know how to fit the pieces together for ourselves. So, fitting the pieces together for everyone involved is an impossible challenge, even for the most proficient problem-solver.

But if each person freely and honestly takes his or her own journey of suffering—and allows others to do the same—then at some point, everyone may be able to walk together in peace again.

Consider the others in your story of suffering. Is there someone that you must release to her or his own journey of suffering?

What might that look like in your relationship?

55

THOSE WHO CAUSED THE PAIN

There is a chance that at least some of the suffering in your life has come through the actions of others—whether one person or several. Let's talk about this.

This subject is a difficult one for many reasons. It is one of the situations we often keep shut away in a box, hoping or assuming it will take care of itself. It won't. And without resolution, it will continually set up roadblocks along your healing journey. At some point, we must come to peace with the kind of relationship we are going to have with the person or people who caused our suffering.

The person who caused the pain may have been a stranger, an acquaintance, or someone very close to you, maybe even a family member. Or there could be a combination of people—some you know and some you don't know. Whatever the case, your relationship with that person or with the people involved has changed forever. So, it is time to talk about how we will respond to those changes.

Who might this be for you? Here are some possibilities to consider:

- A stranger, with no previous connection, who was pulled into a relationship with you based on suffering

- A once trusted person, whether because of your relationship or their position, who you stopped trusting when your expectations were shattered—and yet the nature of the relationship or position still imposes on you some form of loyalty or longing for reconciliation

- A family member who broke your trust in a conflict that would have once been unimaginable but whom you still feel you must protect—because you think you should be loyal to family at all costs

- A friend or family member whose action broke a relationship which you have no desire to repair to its former status

Then, once we determine who this is for us, what do we do? How do we respond to those who have harmed us?

God opens this discussion in His Word and for a very good reason. As our Creator, God knows us very well. He knows that, often, our responses swing from one extreme to another, both of which are unhealthful for our healing.

One such unhealthy response is to take vengeance. Vengeance is the action of paying back evil for the evil that has been done. People, tribes, and even countries often take vengeance on others because of imposed hurt. Vengeance is a common response to hurt. For that reason, God gives instruction like the following:

> Make sure that nobody pays back wrong for wrong (1 Thessalonians 5:15).
>
> Do not take revenge, my dear friends, but leave room for God's wrath (Romans 12:19).
>
> Do not say, "I'll do to them as they have done to me; I'll pay them back for what they did" (Proverbs 24:29).

When someone hurts us, our minds often begin to think about how we can hurt them back. We consider ways that we can make them hurt equally so that they will know our pain. We feel we have the right to exact payback. And yet, God tells us over and over again—do not pay back evil for evil.

There is an inbuilt problem with vengeance. We are never able to "pay back" to the exact amount and with the same emotion and results. Each person will always feel that she has been wronged in a greater way. And so, the need for further vengeance.

God knows that if we continue to repay evil for evil, the only thing we will accomplish is to move from one difficult situation to another—perhaps escalating into a dangerous situation. If every person took revenge, the trouble would never end; the poison would only continue to damage all involved but also grow in intensity.

Further, wrapped up in the emotions of vengeance is the desire for the other person to comprehend the hurt they inflicted on us. With amazement, we look on, as their actions, words, and even facial expressions seem to prove their lack of consciousness to the deep pain and destruction they have caused. But this is yet another moment when we must step back and look at the situation from a different perspective. From our close and emotional viewpoint, it is easy to feel that if there is no immediate vindication, we might become overwhelmed with pain while the other person gets away with evil. But our God sees the situation from a timeless vantage point, in which perfect and complete justice will ultimately happen.

You see, we are to refuse to seek vengeance because we are not capable of carrying it out with justice or rightness. Instead, vengeance only brings us more suffering. But God is capable of bringing perfect justice. And He ultimately does so by bringing His own form of vengeance on those who harm the weak. He works through the legal system or other authorities, or He uses circumstances to bring discipline upon someone in a particular way. And in those instances when we may not see God's justice in our lifetime, we can trust that His justice will come when He makes all things right on His appointed day.

But is It possible to move forward from trauma without seeking, or at least hoping for, vengeance? Without repayment for the hurt that was done, the matter seems unsettled. Isn't that what justice is all about?

Vengeance and justice are not the same. Although we are to refuse the instinct that surfaces to pay back evil that is done to us or to someone we love, that does not mean that it is wrong for justice to be done. Justice is "rightness." A person may be brought to justice under the law or experience the natural consequences of their behavior. This is a part of God's plan in this world. Refusing to seek vengeance does not mean refusing to allow justice to do its job.

And this brings us to another unhealthy response to those who caused us pain—to *cover over* evil. We are not to repay evil with evil, but we are not to *hide* evil either. There are times when a group of people, even a church, will cover the evil done by one of their members. This can be done to protect the reputation of the evil-doer or the group, or it can happen due to an incorrect perception of the evil and how it is impacting the weak. Sometimes, it happens simply to avoid the struggle that comes with uncovering evil. And yet, the condoning or covering of evil is just as incorrect and unwise as seeking vengeance.

Remember that God's heart is for the victim, the abused, the weak, and the oppressed. When we cover up intentional abuse against another person, we put ourselves on the opposite side of God. By protecting the evil, we add to the abuse of the victim.

So, if we do not seek revenge for evil, and we do not cover up evil, what *do* we do?

We speak the truth. And we wait for God to carry out appropriate and right consequences.

God's anger *does* come against those who harm the weak and the oppressed. It *will* come. For these are the ones who hold a special place in His heart.

But if you do wrong, be afraid, for rulers do not bear the sword for no reason. They are God's servants, agents of wrath to bring punishment on the wrongdoer (Romans 13:4).

We can trust our pain and suffering to God. He knows best how to defend us and will bring justice at the right time and in the right manner. It brings great relief and peace when we give up the need to "make someone pay" and place that responsibility into God's hands instead.

We still have much to talk about as we consider our relationships with those who have harmed us. But now, it's time for a bend in the road.

A BEND IN THE ROAD
WHAT KIND OF JUSTICE DO I WANT?

Record your thoughts about vengeance—about the desire to see someone pay, about the deep longing for that person to feel your hurt. This might feel and look *ugly*—you might be unsure if you want to admit to these emotions. But it is part of the cleansing—the cleansing that opens the wound for healing.

Then discuss the kind of justice you want to see for those who have been involved in causing your pain. What does this look like when you set aside vengeance?

As you sit safely under the protection of the shade tree, speak truth.

Then it will be time to move further down the road.

56

WHAT ABOUT FORGIVENESS?

At one point in time, I thought I had completed my writing about suffering and trauma. I lifted my hands in success and mentally filed the task under "accomplished." Until my Traveling Companion began to nudge me, as if to say, *"One more thing. One more topic. One more important part of healing."*

Oh, no! I thought. *The dreaded conversation.*

You see, I was cornered, with my back against the wall. I knew my Good Shepherd's teachings on forgiveness. I knew that it was part of my conversation with Him every time I prayed His prayer: "Forgive my trespasses, *as I forgive* those who trespass against me." I also knew what *un*forgiveness felt like; and although my reasons for it seemed legitimate, it tied me to the pain in a way that felt unhealthy.

And so, I spent some months reading, thinking, and praying about forgiveness. My Good Shepherd stayed with me in the conversation. I discovered that His intentions for me were for my good and for my healing. I also discovered that I had some incorrect ideas about what forgiveness is.

WHAT IS FORGIVENESS?

No matter who caused the harm, how much time passes, or how hard we try to push it aside, eventually we encounter this idea of forgiveness. It just seems to be something that we are expected to do.

Advice comes from many directions: "You should forgive," or "No, it's impossible to forgive," or "You must forgive!" And whenever the recommendation is given, it often comes as a package deal: "Forgive and restore," "Forgive and forget," or "Forgive and move on."

Forgive. It is a word often spoken and heard without full comprehension of its meaning. Even as we read the word *forgiveness*, it conjures up various definitions and expectations in our minds—and this is important because *what we do with forgiveness* is filtered through those expectations.

So, it is best to stop here and clarify our definition of forgiveness. Then you will be able to think through how forgiving might play out in your life. You might even find that you respond differently to the idea of forgiveness once you understand it more clearly.

Let's start with what forgiveness *is*:

> Forgiveness is to remove my focus from the source of the pain and replace it with my awareness of the goodness of God.
>
>> I remain confident of this: I will see the goodness of the LORD in the land of the living. Wait for the LORD; be strong and take heart and wait for the LORD (Psalm 27:13–14).

> Forgiveness is to give up my right to pay back, or seek vengeance for, the harm done to me.
>
>> Do not say, "I'll do to them as they have done to me; I'll pay them back for what they did" (Proverbs 24:29).

> Forgiveness is to release the desire that bad—in general from any source—happens in the life of the offender. In time, forgiveness allows us to accept—without bitterness—good that comes into that person's life.
>
>> "But to you who are listening I say: Love your enemies, do good to those who hate you, bless those who curse you, pray for those who mistreat you" (Luke 6:27–28).

> Forgiveness is to think of the offender as a fellow image-bearer of God, responsible for his or her actions, but also broken by sin just as I am.
>
>> There is no one righteous, not even one . . . for all have sinned and fall short of the glory of God (Romans 3:10, 23).

> Finally, forgiveness is something that happens *inside me*—for my good and for God's glory. God instructs us to forgive because He knows what it will mean in our healing process. When we forgive, we can, in turn, experience God's forgiveness, which allows us to have spiritual healing.
>
>> Bear with each other and forgive one another if any of you has a grievance against someone. Forgive as the LORD forgave you (Colossians 3:13).

WHAT ARE THE REQUIREMENTS OF FORGIVENESS?

Often, when someone recommends forgiving, they promote it as a package deal: "Forgive and restore," "Forgive and forget," or "Forgive and move on." But this "package deal" perception of forgiveness usually makes us want to run—or hang our heads in shame.

The very nature of the words *restore, forget,* and *move on* ring with pretense and hypocrisy; we feel the "rub" of insincerity that links these actions to forgiveness, as if they are a required formula. But notice that none of these words are used in the previous descriptions of forgiveness. This is because they are not actually a required part of forgiving someone.

With that in mind, let's talk about some of the misconceptions of what forgiveness *requires*.

FORGIVENESS DOES NOT REQUIRE RESTORATION

Some may say, "Forgiveness is commanded." This is a true statement, and yet, wrapped up in that statement is often the expectation, the requirement, that we restore a previous relationship—or at least a relationship status.

This is a dangerous misunderstanding of forgiveness—both its definition and its purpose. The dangerous part is to *require restoration* as a part of forgiveness. To impose restoration as an obligation impedes the real experience of forgiveness that takes us further down the path of healing.

> *In fact, people often avoid forgiveness solely because
> they believe restoration is one of the requirements.*

To "restore" is to return something back to its original condition.

Suppose a man is president of a bank. His job is to protect the money that people put into the bank. So, everyone trusts him to protect their accounts. Then one day, they discover he has been making unwise financial decisions, and money has been lost as a result. They speak to him about it, and he apologizes. Then all continues as before. Later, funds come up missing again, and when he is confronted this time, the man explains that the losses are due to bookkeeping errors.

Eventually, the people discover that the "trusted" president was actually stealing money from the bank all along. In fact, he had been doing this for years. Even as he claimed to be protecting and caring for what they had entrusted to him, he was taking what was not his and using it for himself. He was a thief.

Over time, the people might forgive the man for the harm he did to them (and remember our definition of forgiveness), but if they are wise, they will probably not put him in charge of their money again! He lost the privilege of holding that responsibility when he broke a particular trust related to that relationship of honesty and protection. So, his former position of responsibility and privilege cannot be restored.

The same is true in your life. The nature of the original relationship you held with your offender, combined with your level of trust and the severity of their offense, all contribute to how possible it is to restore that original relationship. But forgiving a person who has harmed you *does not require* that you place yourself back under his or her control; it *does not even require* that you put your trust back in that person.

This is particularly true when there has been physical, emotional, or sexual assault or abuse. Moving toward an attitude of forgiveness does not require that you put the relationship back together with the same level of trust and privileges as before. Particularly in the case of physical or sexual abuse, a very clear boundary of trust has been broken that almost certainly has changed that relationship forever. Your protection most likely requires separation from the one who broke that trust and became a perpetrator rather than a person you expected to be safe with.

Sadly, many who have suffered abuse avoid the idea of forgiveness because they have been told that forgiveness is dependent on their willingness to restore the abusive relationship. They do not feel comfortable being in a relationship with the person who has harmed them, and so they assume forgiveness is not an option for them. Their *correct sense of self-protection* then gets rewritten by others to be a spiritual shortcoming—an unwillingness to forgive.

The conclusion either brings a sense of defeat and shame onto the abused, or it pressures him or her to give in to the unwise choice of returning to a situation of harm. When forgiveness is evidenced in this way, it not only promotes a false idea of what it means to forgive but also brings with it the potential for more serious harm.

Worse, there are times when the requirement of forgiveness is used as manipulation of the abused. "Say you forgive me," the abuser says. "You must. It is what God says to do." So, the relationship is "put back together," and the abuse continues, with further such requirements for forgiveness. And the abused person becomes stuck in this devastating cycle. Months or years later, if the relationship is finally severed and the conversation of forgiveness once again includes the expectation of restoration, the abused will avoid even the idea of forgiveness at all costs. And understandably so.

With that said, there are many times when restoring a relationship *is* possible. Perhaps both persons are willing to build that relationship on a new foundation—because the relationship is valuble to both. Going back to attempt to untangle all the ins and outs of the inflicted hurt most often does not lead to restoration, but further misunderstanding. And so, we want to be careful not to withhold restoration of a relationship *for the sake of vengeance or bitterness.*

The potential for restoration of relationship is directly related to the type of offense. We most often seek to heal a relationship to some level. However, there are times when restoration is not the best option or even a healthy option for the one who has suffered. In these situations, it is important to understand that, even without restoration, *the obedient act of forgiveness is still possible.*

FORGIVENESS DOES NOT REQUIRE REPENTANCE

In many instances, the combination of repentance and forgiveness that leads to restoration can be appropriate and right. We should not run from this possibility out of fear or bitterness. God has written beautiful stories of healed relationships as only He can do, and we rejoice in these precious moments. At the same time, *repentance is not required* for forgiveness to happen.

> *This is important, because many people unnecessarily avoid forgiveness when their offender has not repented.*

So, what does it mean to repent? To feel sorry? Express regret? Have a change of heart? To repent is to change one's mind—even one's direction. If we are going one direction and we repent, we turn and go the opposite direction. In that sense, repentance is more than words and promises; there is evidence when there is true repentance.

The evidence, however, often takes time to be revealed. So, we encounter this struggle: *Is the person truly repenting or simply regretful?* we wonder. *Is he playing a part to convince me?* Or, *Does she really understand how she hurt me?* It is difficult to discern the offender's response, because we cannot see the heart.

In understanding the definition of forgiveness, however, we see that the offender's heart status does not affect our ability to forgive. We see that *forgiveness is possible even if that person never repents.* The act of forgiveness is something that happens in *me*—for *my* good—independent of another person's heart, actions, or expectations, so I can forgive that person even if he never says the words I want to hear.

Another important truth is that our forgiveness of the person who did wrong is not connected to that person's *spiritual* forgiveness. Only God can forgive sin. Spiritual forgiveness is between that person and God.

Finally, when we forgive, we, in turn, can receive God's forgiveness, which gives us spiritual healing. Each person's choice is her own; each person's spiritual healing is between him and God. Our choice to forgive nurtures our relationship with God.

Now, let's look at some other things that forgiveness is *not*.

WHAT FORGIVENESS IS *NOT*

In defining forgiveness thus far, we have considered what forgiveness is and discussed some misconceptions around what forgiveness requires. Now it is time to think about what forgiveness is *not*.

Forgiveness is *not* something we should offer out of loyalty or because we feel someone "deserves" or "demands" it. In this case it is often the words "I forgive you" that the offender wants to hear. If you are feeling obligated to forgive for any of these reasons, be aware that it may be due to manipulation and that such "forgiveness" will only contribute to further pain rather than healing.

Forgiveness does *not* mean that what the person did was okay or that we deserved that harm. It might feel to us that if we forgive, then we will minimize or make light of the suffering the person inflicted. This is not true. God never takes the suffering of the oppressed lightly.

Forgiveness does *not* mean we need to stay loyal to or under the control of someone who repeatedly harms us.

Forgiveness does not mean that we protect the abuser from justice or discipline that God rightly brings. We do not seek vengeance; however, we do allow God's justice.

Forgiving someone does *not* mean we are responsible for that person's healing.

Forgiving someone does *not* require restoring a former relationship to its previous status when that relationship is harmful to us.

Understanding and personalizing these layers of *forgiveness*—what it is, what it is not, and what its requirements look like—will likely take time. We might even think of it as "growing into" the ability to forgive. This process can happen naturally as we come closer to being at peace with the event and rediscovering hope—and further from a life that revolves around the pain of the past. It can happen as we live out the courage we are discovering along this journey of healing. It might even happen on the next bend in the road.

A BEND IN THE ROAD

WHAT ABOUT FORGIVENESS?

Forgiveness is. Forgiveness is not. Only once we have a clear depiction of forgiveness can we consider how it might come to reality in our own situations. This is why the previous conversation made important clarifications.

So, what have you believed about forgiveness? Perhaps, at one time, you determined that forgiveness would be an impossible reality in your life. Perhaps others have attached so many requirements to forgiveness that you have not been able to safely and truthfully consider the possibility. Take some time to consider your own experiences with and impressions of forgiveness. Write them down here.

Then write down how any misconceptions you had were clarified by the previous conversation.

57

FORGIVENESS AS A PART OF RESOLUTION

So, what's the big deal with forgiveness? Why even be concerned with the idea, let alone take time to consider it so carefully?

The conversation about forgiveness is important because, without it, we remain obligated and indebted to the suffering. Do you remember when we talked about "coming to peace" with suffering? This discussion of forgiveness is a critical part of that. Let me show you an example.

If you are like me, there are probably times when a situation feels unresolved. Yes, you have moved on in a variety of ways. But when you think of the person who harmed you or offended you, the mood that hovers and even encompasses you, if you had to label it, might be called "not resolved." It feels toxic. There is no sense of peace to be found.

In these moments, what are we anticipating? What are we waiting for? We have already discovered that we cannot change what has happened. Life is as it is now. Perhaps, we are waiting for some initiative on the other person's part? But what could they do that would truly resolve and bring peace to our pain?

The resolution, the invitation for peace, must come from us . . . to us.

Our desire is to move forward, *away from* the negative control of the suffering. But an unforgiving response to relationships can hold us in the grip of the suffering. As we cling to our anger to prove the intensity of our pain, we allow ourselves to be bound together in our suffering with the one who caused it.

So, forgiveness becomes a powerful impetus in our healing:

- We forgive to keep a correct perspective of our own need for forgiveness.

- We forgive so that our anger and fear do not lead to bitterness that takes over our lives.

- We forgive to experience one more release from the negative control of suffering.

- We forgive to know the peace of obedience to the One who forgives us.

- We forgive so that we may fully express the image of God in us.

Further, we discover that forgiveness is dependent on only one person—and that person is us. We must give ourselves permission to release that hold. Release the bitterness. Release the expectation of that "something" that will make it right.

You will be amazed by how much mental time and energy and emotional strength become available once you release your connection to the source of the pain into God's care.

Is this a one-time "I forgive" moment? Likely not. Forgiveness usually needs revisiting. We reach a moment of forgiveness and find peace for some time. But after a while, we find ourselves sliding back into a desire for vengeance or allowing bitterness to hold us in an unhealthy place. "I forgive" is often a starting point that means "I am in the forgiving process." That is a good place to be.

Remember what forgiveness is. Remember what forgiveness is not.

Then, strengthened by this clarity, intentionally reclaim your peace and sense of well-being, which have been eroded by events, emotions, and expectations—whether for the first time or at any other time during your forgiveness journey.

Peace sometimes comes from the most unexpected places.

FORGIVENESS

Forgiveness is not identified by forgetfulness,
but it is evidenced by release.

Forgiveness is not proven by restoration,
but it is perceptible by peace.

Forgiveness is not something I give.
Forgiveness is a mystery that I embrace.

It is an invitation to untangle myself from the grip of
bitterness, shame, and fear
that brutally holds me to the past.

By embracing forgiveness,
I am able to fully express the image of God in me.

By embracing forgiveness,
I am released—truly free to move forward with peace.

Forgiveness is a gift to me from God—for my good and for His glory.

A BEND IN THE ROAD

WHERE AM I ON MY JOURNEY OF FORGIVENESS?

Reflect on where you feel you are in this process of forgiveness. Write down your thoughts, your concerns, your intentions.

Wasted. Spoiled. Tainted. Ruined.

Many of us have used such words, whether in our speech or just in our minds, to describe certain periods of time from our past—periods of days, weeks, even years. The emotions of those words leak into our current lives in the form of disappointment, bitterness, and apprehension about the future.

So, let's replace these words with another: *Reclaim*. This word means "to return value to something or to make it new; to restore purpose."

Through the years, God has reclaimed various things in my life:

> places I didn't want to return to,
>
> times of year or seasons,
>
> songs that were difficult to hear.

God has reclaimed these things by proving to me that it was not that place, that time, or that song that caused the suffering. These were only small descriptive details of that painful time. He has also reclaimed things, places, and even people as they have come to be woven anew into my story.

Reclaim.

Here is an example. Perhaps, your suffering brought loss through family members in a way that the very idea of family itself has become a connection to pain. Now, faced with the prospect of interacting with other family members or the potential for gaining a new family, you are tempted to hide from or reject the possibility. God can reclaim the idea of family so that you can *reclaim possession of the idea that joy is possible* through family interactions in your future.

I have seen God reclaim something as simple as a piece of clothing and something as complex as a relationship. He specializes in restoring value and purpose. He has a way of replacing negative with positive and replacing waste with blessing, as shown in the following verses:

> I called on your name, LORD. . . . You heard my plea. . . .
> You came near when I called you, and you said, "Do not
> fear." You, LORD, took up my case; you redeemed my life
> (Lamentations 3:55–58).

The negative effects of suffering whisper words of waste and ruin into our lives. But God's precious work of redemption (reclaiming) speaks the possibility of value and joy into those moments and things that we once associated with our pain. These things can be reclaimed—given new value, given new purpose!

And what is our part in that process? We adjust our vision. We embrace hope. We open ourselves to the *possibility of joy or blessing* in areas that once held only pain. With our eyes on I AM, we lift open hands—and we let Him do His mysterious work.

We are at a bend in the road.

A BEND IN THE ROAD

RECLAIMED

Make note of anything in your life that has been reclaimed after negative connections threatened to hold it hostage. These are precious gifts on our journey of healing. These are places where God has reclaimed our story.

Now, what is there that brings pain and could possibly be reclaimed?

Up to this point, our conversation has focused on suffering that is beyond our control—natural disasters, physical Illness, abuse, intentional harm by others, life events, and so on.

But there is another kind of suffering. I know because I have experienced it. This suffering comes through direct disobedience to God's principles and commands. Please stay with me. Again, I tell you first what is *not* true about this statement so that we can move on to focus on what *is* true.

- It is *not* true that all suffering happens because of a particular sin or disobedience.
- It is *not* true that if we are obedient, we will avoid suffering.
- It *is*, however, true that direct and intentional disobedience often results in suffering.

Let's talk about this. God, as our Creator, gives us principles and commands to follow that are good and right for us. When He gives instruction, it is not for the purpose of imposing His control or spoiling our fun. He knows what will harm us, what will bring hardship and suffering; He also knows what will promote our peace and safety. So, to intentionally turn our backs on Him and make a choice that goes against His principles is to walk into the potential for great suffering. That suffering comes because of the natural consequences of the action; it is the reasonable pain that comes when something is harmful to us.

Don't steal. Don't murder. Don't speak untruth. Don't commit adultery. Don't wish for what belongs to someone else.

These are just a few of the instructions that God gives to us *because He knows the suffering—to us and others—that comes when they are not followed.* His guidelines provide strong protection for us. When we make the decision to ignore the guidelines, we step out of that protection—and that can be a frightening and grievous place to be. Suddenly, we are open to the natural consequences. We usually find ourselves making more wrong choices to try to avoid those consequences. One thing leads to another, and sooner or later, we feel the pain.

This suffering is not caused by someone else's choice but is the result of our own choice. What do we do with this kind of suffering? Well, I will tell you from experience what we *don't* do.

- Avoiding the issue that caused the suffering, hoping it will just go away, doesn't work.

- Covering up or justifying our actions, which leads to more sin, doesn't work.

- Doing good works to offset the disobedience doesn't work.

So, we are left with only one answer:

We turn to the Creator who made us,

the I Am, who is trustworthy,

the Ruler of All, who is all-powerful, all-knowing, all-present, and all-good,

the Good Shepherd, who protects and shows us the way,

the Savior, who can now save us.

But when I sin, should I not run *from* Him? That is what untruth will whisper in your ear. But the truth is that He is the One to whom we should run—as quickly as possible. He is our safe place.

I remember the overwhelming deluge of emotion when my sin was fully exposed: despair, fear, guilt. Yes, it was a gut-wrenching moment of awareness—awareness of self-condemnation and self-defense; it touched parts of me that I did not even know existed. And yet, it also felt right. It was good. This is called repentance. It is a moment of agreement with our Creator that He was right, and I was wrong.

It is in this moment that we come to know ourselves a bit better. We see our weaknesses. We see our short-sightedness. We see our arrogance. We see our frailty. We see our need. We see our sin—our rebellion against God. To be honest, I had never seen my need as clearly as I did in those moments of anguish. I had never felt so desperate for mercy.

This is a good place to be. It is in this place, where we see our own inability to make things right, that we come face to face with Him—and with all that He has attempted to prove to us about His love for us. We find that His mercy (not receiving what we justly deserve) covers the guilt and fear, while His grace (receiving blessing that we do not deserve) introduces us to unexpected peace and the possibility of a reclaimed future.

A new awareness comes, where . . .

> despair is touched by hope,
>
> fear melts into peace,
>
> guilt is softened by love, and
>
> it is clear that a mystery beyond expression is unfolding.

Yet, for me, what followed was deep depression. I felt His mercy; but I was consumed by my unworthiness, my sense of failure. How could I go forward? How could I raise my head? I was undone. I was determined to sit in despondency. That was where I belonged. And that was where I remained.

Until my precious Traveling Companion came and sat with me. He explained to me that I had been just as in need of Him *before* this great failure. That, even when I thought I was doing things well, I desperately needed His cleansing. That left to myself, I had always been in danger. He assured me that His mercy was big enough to handle this moment of wrongdoing and waywardness. He assured me that His forgiveness was intended for such a time as this. He told me this was an opportunity for me to see the truth in a way I had never recognized before. The truth of my weakness. My shortsightedness. My arrogance. My frailty. My need. And my vulnerability.

He lifted my face so that I could see Him and my heart so that I could trust Him. And I heard something like this:

> Blessed is the one whose transgressions are forgiven, whose sins
> are covered. (Psalm 32:1)

Blessed = Content. Yes, even joyful. There is pure joy in the awareness of being forgiven. It is as if a burden is lifted, and the remaining awareness is of peace, calm, and protection once again.

So, do all the consequences of disobedience disappear? No. There may be consequences that linger. But after repenting and receiving forgiveness, we are no longer lost in the dangerous wilderness. Our Good Shepherd can show us the way out of any challenges and pain that may remain.

Perhaps, this conversation of sin and repentance is new to you. Perhaps you have simply lived with the conflict that goes on inside—times of guilt followed by times of feeling good about yourself; times of weakness after times of determination. It might be a new thought to you that this conflict is because of our need to be in a right relationship with our Creator, who is also our Traveling Companion, the I Am. This need has been here, however, since the beginning of time.

Our tendency toward disobedience began soon after creation. Adam and Eve made a choice to disobey the one instruction God had given to them. This ended tragically in a broken relationship with their precious Creator and companion. In fact, it was then that suffering entered our world. And since that time, as we discovered in our earlier conversation, the world is broken.

The truth is that *our* relationship with our Creator is broken as well. Deep down, our souls sense it. We might not be able to consciously put our finger on the problem; we just know that something is wrong. We like to think that we can fix things on our own, and we certainly try. Oh, the many ways we attempt to settle the anxieties and turmoil within, thinking there is something we can do to bring peace. But our efforts result only in short-term moments of settledness—until, again, we are undone.

But we have discovered that our God is good and that He loves us in a way we have never been loved by anyone else. So, that fractured relationship was as painful for Him as for us.

As our Creator, He also knew how we would long for peace, often not comprehending why it seems to elude us. And being the I Am, He made a way for the relationship to be restored. That restoration comes through Jesus Christ—through His life on this earth, His death on the cross, and His resurrection, by which He destroyed death.

Upheaval. Uncertainty. Disobedience. Disconnect. Only God Himself can provide a way to heal our relationship with Him. All along our journey, we have been looking for a way forward, for truth and new life. And here is the source:

> Jesus answered, "I am the way and the truth and the life. No one comes to the Father except through me." (John 14:6)

> Therefore, if anyone is in Christ, the new creation has come: The old has gone, the new is here! (2 Corinthians 5:17)

Now, even after rebellion and disobedience, we are known, seen, and loved in a profound way by this perfect and trusted Traveling Companion. We can take all our disobedience, the intentional and the unintentional, and run to Him. We can tell Him that we cannot fix it. We can lay down our fears, our doubts, our accusations. We can shed our tears of repentance and humble ourselves, releasing our pride and self-sufficiency and the "I-can-do-its." And we can be assured: there is courage and peace on the other side of repentance.

In this way, the door opens to a healed relationship with God. And this is why He is such a perfect Traveling Companion. For all the pain and uncertainty of other relationships and events in my life, I can have peace with my Creator and the profound awareness of His mercy and grace and presence with me on the journey.

Now, here we are, at a bend in the road.

A BEND IN THE ROAD

A CONVERSATION

This journey is not an easy one; we knew that when we began. Perhaps, like me, you have a particular area of suffering that needs repentance and restoration. Or, perhaps, you simply need to have an intimate conversation with the One who can forgive and heal perfectly. He wants to be your companion, your Savior. He knows you need Him. Run to Him. Pour out your thoughts on this page.

Here we are—well into our journey.

We have encountered multiple bends in the road,
discovering truth,
gathering awareness of value,
discarding deception.

Some things we hold close as a treasure,
others we have left on the roadside.
We are sorting things out.
Unraveling.
Resolving.

Not one of us would describe this path as easy.

Yet, even with the intensity,
there is a sense of relief that is growing "slowly by slowly."

We are becoming familiar with our suffering,
gaining perspective of good and evil,
writing a new narrative that includes beauty.

And there is an awareness that we are, in fact,
moving through healing,
as
fear moves closer to courage,
vulnerability gives way to strength, and
despair encounters hope.

PROTECTION FOR OUR WELL-BEING

We are encouraged
by forward movement
and the freedom that is budding.
Yet, we welcome the tenacious
tethers and protective boundaries
that hold us during sudden turmoil,
even renewed threats of destruction.

61
TETHERS

A *tether* is something that holds an object to keep it from moving too far from a particular location. It holds the object within certain bounds, often for the purpose of keeping it safe.

Chances are, we have felt *tethered* to our suffering, or some portion of it. For that reason, much of our journey has been a movement away from that captivity, away from being held within the bounds of that moment of crisis.

The freedom we have gained to move forward from the grip and control of trauma is a welcome breath of fresh air. We do not want to sail aimlessly away, however, or we may end up haphazardly floating toward confusion or even retraumatization. All of us know how easy it is to make a choice only to become consumed by fears and emotions, which then nudge us in a different direction. We are also easily distracted by the expectations of others. Or we read a book or attend a seminar, and off we go once again!

So, even though we are encouraged by freedom and forward movement, we need something to keep us within certain bounds of security. We need some *safety tethers*.

> Like strong ropes that hold a kayak to the dock in tumultuous wind, we want our tethers to be tenacious and unbreakable, holding us during sudden turmoil, confusion, and even renewed threats of destruction.

Below, I have identified some good and right tethers. *These* tethers are strong yet gentle; they are truthful, dependable, and unaffected by our emotions or others' expectations. These tethers are for our protection, for our good. We welcome them. You will notice that each one is attached to God. *We now know why, don't we? The only faithful, dependable hope to which we can hold unswervingly*—we want our tethers attached to that!

OUR SAFETY TETHERS

God's love: We are suspicious of love as a tether because, in truth, many of us do not trust it. We have found it untrustworthy in some situations. Hear me out. God's love is different from the love of all others. He loved you before you ever knew of Him. He set His heart on you. You can do nothing to earn His love or to make Him stop loving you. God's love is pure, good, and just. God's love is a perfect tether, because it began with Him, and it is eternal.

God's presence: One of our heart's desires is for someone to be with us —really *with* us. In our pain, in our suffering, in our longings, and to the depth of our souls. God's presence is different from any other. He never runs out of time or interest. He never runs low on patience. In His presence, you are not at the mercy of chaos or human will. God is with you in your suffering. Even when you push Him away, He remains. God's sure presence with you is a tether that holds you when you feel abandoned and unseen.

God's goodness: *Good* is a term that, for most of us, lost much of its meaning as we scrambled for answers in our suffering. For many of us, what we thought was good exploded into evil. But there is *true* goodness in our lives. You may have been pondering this unique goodness and perhaps even beginning to trust it when you do *not* see it. It is God's pure and right goodness, and it is a tether that holds us, even in the chaos of doubt and despair.

Identity in God: Although trauma is a part of our story, it is not our identity. Further, when we attempt to restore or reestablish our identity as we imagined it was before our crisis, we make unwise decisions. The truth is that your *true* identity is not what you imagined it to be before. It also cannot be destroyed by abuse and pain. Your true identity, as a unique and intentional creation of God, tethers you. It holds you when uncertainty calls you to run after other assurances.

Value from God: The ability to make good choices is jeopardized when we do not consider our personal value in the equation. Fortunately, we have value that is not diminished by the events that have happened to us. The value given to you by God is a tether that holds you safe whenever you are tempted to seek value in harmful ways.

The truth about suffering: We are now able to recognize many of the threats, lies, and accusations that trauma uses to hold us in its grip. We have also been warned that trauma wants to consume us. Going a step further, knowing the truth about suffering is a tether that keeps us from being carried away by these waves of trauma. The truth about suffering is that it is not the bad guy. Suffering also is temporary. Oh, it feels like it has settled in for good. But it does come and go, both in its presence and its intensity.

A sure hope: We have discovered that much of our previous hoping was actually wishful thinking and that, for this reason, we were swept away by suffering and disappointment. Now, we find it difficult to set our confidence on anything. Yet, the great I Am is the one and only sure hope that cannot be destroyed, will never fail, and will not disappoint. This sure hope is a tether that holds us from wandering off after unrealistic or even unwise wishes seem to go unfulfilled.

These tethers are good, powerful, and capable; they never change, they never lose strength, and their truth is eternal. If we go wandering out of the bounds of their safety, it is not because the tethers broke under stress; it is because we did not stay connected to them.

Let me explain. When you remember to keep your focus on the tethers of truth described above, they can hold you in clarity and safety when a trigger threatens to send you reeling into paralyzing and destructive panic.

It is helpful to us that we have a pioneer who has experienced this same threat—and come through that experience with perfection.

Because Jesus lived in this world, He experienced His own journey of suffering. He was tempted often and in the same ways that we are—tempted to abandon His true purpose and embrace false promises and enticements. In that dangerous place, He fixed His eyes on truth that enabled Him to endure to the completion of His task. He focused on the tethers that would hold Him.

Listen to this message about Jesus, which gives us a profound and perfect example of what it means to keep our eyes fixed on truth—from His perspective and from ours:

> Let us throw off everything that hinders and the sin that so easily entangles. And let us run with perseverance . . . fixing our eyes on Jesus, the pioneer and perfecter of faith. For the joy set before him he endured the cross, scorning its shame, and sat down at the right hand of the throne of God. (Hebrews 12:1–2)

These words of promise and assurance are powerful and relevant. Let's look at the second part of the verse first, which reminds us that:

- suffering is temporary, with a beginning and an end;
- suffering can be endured; and
- it is the hope of the "joy to come" that helps us endure.

The first part of the verse reminds us that Jesus, as the pioneer, is the one on whom we can fix our eyes, the one to whom we can tether.

These truths themselves are the safety tethers. However, in the moment when we are triggered, we are often not thinking clearly. Our gaze is easily distracted, often wandering away from the truth. And it is then that we lose our connection to the safety tethers.

It can be helpful to have a tangible object in such moments that will capture your attention and refocus your gaze on the truth. It might be a particular bracelet, a string of prayer beads, a piece of needlework, a printed picture, or a verse. This item, whatever you choose, is not to be worshiped and is not strong enough in itself to hold you firmly; however, it can help you to "reconnect" by reminding you of the powerful tethers that hold you in safety.

The tethers are there. How will you use them? Let's consider this more at this next bend in the road.

A BEND IN THE ROAD

TETHERS

Commit the safety tethers to memory. Write them on a small card or piece of paper for a reminder. Which of the safety tethers are most powerful in your journey of healing?

Choose a tangible object to be your connection point to the tethers when the panic and fear set in. Write about it here or draw a picture. If it is a verse, write it here.

YOUR VALUE FROM GOD

GOD'S LOVE

GOD'S PRESENCE

GOD'S GOODNESS

YOUR IDENTITY IN GOD

A SURE HOPE

THE TRUTH ABOUT SUFFERING

62

I NEED

At times,
like a brilliant & strong sunflower,
I burst forth . . . unhindered,
face open to the heavens,
expressing promise, joy, and hope.

At others,
I am downtrodden,
entangled by vines that grip,
draining my strength and courage.
I need a caregiver,
One who tends; One who lifts; One who prunes.
One who sets boundaries
Here and no more . . .

"The LORD will guide you always;
he will satisfy your needs in a sun-scorched
land
and will strengthen your frame.
You will be like a well-watered garden,
like a spring whose waters never fail."
(Isaiah 58:11)

63

TRUTH AND UNTRUTH IN OUR GARDEN

This contemplative journey is pressing you forward in ways you might not even recognize. For instance, at each bend in the road, you have encountered a challenge. You have considered the information presented and then, in some form or another, you have responded to questions such as, "Do I see this guidance as truth? Am I willing to accept the invitation, embrace the suggestions, and apply the conclusions in my own life?" If you willingly moved forward, you then applied *truth* to your own narrative—and with that same effort, *you uncovered untruth.*

And so, with each bend in the road, you have been faced with *truth and untruth.*

Often, it is a challenge to discern between the two. Trauma whispers untruth, which often sounds like it is sympathizing with us, taking our side. But when we observe more carefully, we find that it is either holding us in a place of captivity and confining us—or leading us down paths that would destroy rather than heal.

On the other hand, truth challenges the trauma, opening the door to release us from trauma's captivity and showing us a way forward. But this often leads us into unfamiliar territory. It challenges our status quo, prompting us to move away from that place we have lived for so long. That might be a place of fear, anger, or guilt, but it has seemed a logical, unavoidable, and even somewhat comfortable place to stay. Until now.

And then, there is the clean-up: once we identify untruth, we must remove it.

For this reason, we are about to discover one of our strongest tools for healing—*the ability to remove untruth and, in its place, establish truth.*

OUR GARDEN

Imagine that you have been given a small garden plot. The plot has been left alone for several years, so it is full of weeds. You decide that you are going to plant flowers in your plot. Do you simply add new flower seeds to the ground? No. You must first clear out the weeds. Because if you add the flower seeds to the ground as it is, the weeds will quickly and certainly choke out the new plants. After all, the weeds have been there for quite some time. They have taken ownership of the ground—and they are tenacious! Even if flowers do grow, before long, the flowers will no longer be seen. They will be consumed by the weeds, and the ground will return to its former state.

Our journey of suffering is like that too. It is like a garden plot that we have been given to tend. We want our garden to be a place of peace and beauty and productivity, but the negative effects of suffering—the untruths—have already taken root there and grown prolifically into weeds.

At this stage, if we simply plant new seeds, the trauma will attempt to choke out any new growth we may see.

First, we must uproot the weeds.

As we move toward healing, we cannot simply plant truths among the untruths. Those untruths have been there for some time, and they have become strong and familiar to us, controlling our reasoning and our very lives. We must pull them out as we discern them, or they will eventually choke out any growth we have seen.

So far on this journey, our bends in the road have helped us to identify and plant some seeds of truth—and with that same effort, we have identified and uncovered roots of untruth. Now that we are at our next bend in the road, it is time to . . .

identify the *untruth* and remove it

and

identify the truth and provide all that it needs to grow strong.

We dare not allow both to coexist in our garden; we have come too far to have our growth undone.

A BEND IN THE ROAD
TENDING OUR GARDEN

Let's work on our gardens.

When you look at your garden on the next page, you will see that the flowers and weeds are growing together, sometimes intertwined. If you want your flowers to survive and thrive, you cannot simply leave the garden this way and hope for the best. It would be wiser to identify the weeds so that you can uproot them.

To start this process, think carefully on both the truths and untruths you have discovered. To discern one from the other, you might have to exercise scientific logic, using "If-then" statements, such as "If *this*, then *that*." We have a tendency to collect various "truths" from different places —from this person, that book, or this new program—but if we look closely, we will find that many of these "truths" contradict. So we must reason, "If *this* is true, then *that* cannot be true," or said another way, "If *this* is truth, then *that* must be untruth."

It can also help to discern truth from untruth by thinking about the things that have helped you along your journey—such as discoveries you have made that have given you strength or tools you have tried that have provided for your defense during times of attack—things that are "tried and *true*." Then, think of the untruths they need to displace.

Trauma is extremely clever with the untruth that it whispers. In some untruth, we can even find a small root of truth—but it has been bent and twisted until it can no longer be trusted to guide our actions. So we must think carefully, following each inclination to its conclusion—is it truth that strengthens or untruth that debilitates?

Test the words and ideas that begin to float around inside your head, discerning where they lead you. Do they steer you toward healing or toward defeat? Do they sound like words from your Creator and Savior, the I Am—or not?

There are many possibilities. Below are just a few ideas of what untruth might sound like.

Words from your own mind:

"If I got myself into this mess, I am going to have to learn to live with it."

"It's my responsibility to keep my family together and happy."

"If only I would have done things differently, this would not have happened."

Words from others:

"You are suffering because you are guilty."

"If you love me, then you should not care about justice."

"You are making too big of a deal about this."

"If only you would have done things the way I told you to, this would not have happened."

Using colored pencils, label the weeds in the garden on the next page with words and phrases that capture the the *untruths* that you uncover. Be very specific.

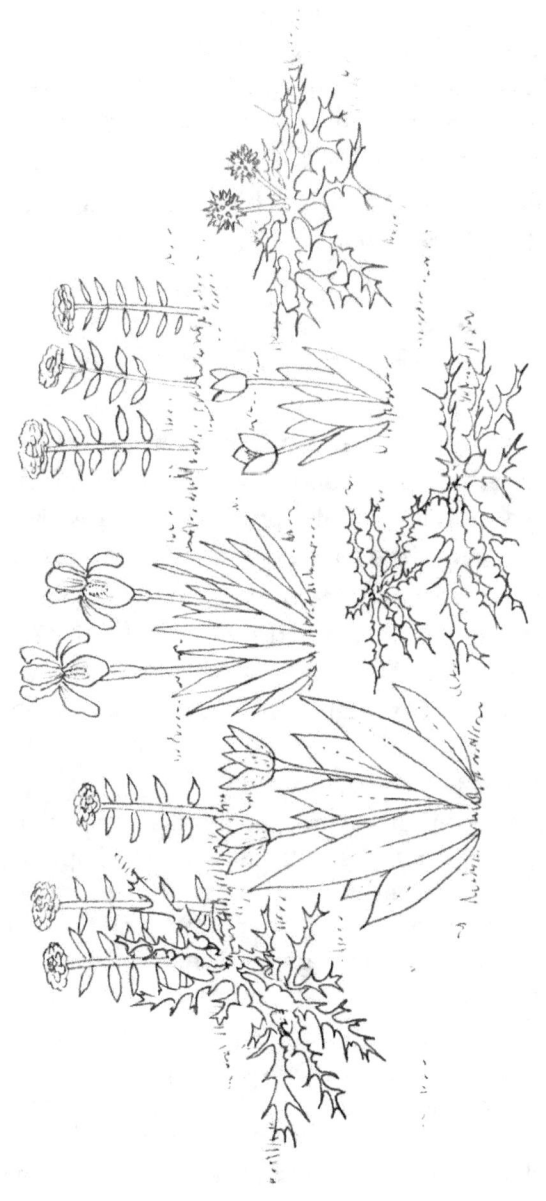

And now, for truth—truth that you have been discovering on your journey. Sometimes, identifying truth is as simple as speaking the reverse of the untruth. In other words, you might look at one of your labeled weeds and write down its opposite. (If a weed is labeled "It is my responsibility to keep everyone happy," you could label a flower with "It is *not* my responsibility to keep everyone happy.") Other times, we must present truth as a new thought, unrelated to the weeds that hold us back (for example, "My life is not at the mercy of the suffering.")

As you consider what truths to add, be honest, practical, and specific:

Add truths that relate to your unique situation.

Add truths that you can realistically apply to your life.

Take time now to write words and phrases of truth in your garden with confidence; words of truth must be planted with conviction.

Planting truth is a strong protection. The truth spreads its roots and becomes established. It takes ownership of our lives and sets us free to grow. As it does, the untruth begins to wilt away. It is proven to be a deceiver and a threat to our well-being, and its grip, which has held us for so long, loosens.

Truth. Untruth. The two cannot grow agreeably in your garden. One must be uprooted. The other must be planted and tended with care and attention.

We know which way this must go. Truth must win. Yes, some untruth is difficult to remove—it has been familiar to us, even as it caused harm—but we are stronger now. We can do this. So, get your clippers and your shovel, and let's do some clean-up.

Go back to the weeds that you have labeled and place an X next to the ones that you want to uproot first. Just keep the clippers and shovel handy, because weeds grow back. Yes, even after I have uprooted some weeds, I find myself feeling anxious—and when I take the time to understand why, I realize it is because I am once again listening to the same old untruth that used to plague me, time and again.

As long as we are in this fallen world, tending our garden will require routine maintenance—but the more we identify and root out the weeds, the more able we will be to maintain new growth. So return to this bend in the road as often as you need, as you identify newly revealed truths and untruths on your continued journey. Use this visual expression to help you in the actual tending of your life garden. You will sense the growth of peace as you carefully discern the flowers and the weeds.

64

DISCOVERING THE NEED FOR PROTECTION

One of the most important steps on our journey has been to learn to acknowledge suffering—to see it, feel it, become familiar with it, and yet, to *set boundaries* that allow us to look at the suffering on our own terms and within our own timetables. This step enabled us to stop hiding from suffering.

Then we became aware of the tactics of trauma. Some may have believed that such awareness would increase our fear of suffering; but, in fact, it only *strengthened our boundaries* against the accusations and threats that trauma would try to send stealthily across our path of healing.

And trauma will continue to try to launch such threats against us—because trauma, left to its own devices, would gladly consume us. This is why, now, as we begin to build up our gardens of truth and untruth, we must become even more aware of trauma's tactics and set up further protective boundaries.

You have started the diligent work of identifying and uprooting untruth in your garden and planting truth in its place. As you continue to work on making your garden a peaceful and thriving environment, you will begin to see growth, productivity, and beauty—and you will want to ensure this environment remains protected against any threat to its well-being. The first step in building up this boundary of protection is to identify the potential threats.

By this point, we might assume that we should know how to identify the threats. But, as usual, trauma often keeps us guessing with its confusing tactics. Its threats to our garden are multidirectional—meaning we will need to keep harm *out* and keep good and beauty *in*. They also take on various appearances—sometimes entering boldly and other times reaching quietly and furtively into areas where they are unwelcome.

However, we can more easily identify these threats by understanding the two main maneuvers that trauma uses to cause harm to our gardens:

- It instills and feeds our fear at times when it is *unnecessary*. It does this by imposing a perceived threat from someone or something that actually has neither the intention nor the desire to hurt us.

- It pacifies our concern for harm at times when that concern *is necessary*. It does this by talking us out of our uneasiness with a perceived threat, telling us that "this person," "that event," or "that action" would never hurt us and, therefore, we must be imagining it.

In addition to identifying the threats themselves, we must also identify areas of weakness around our gardens. Perhaps, there are areas where courage and peace are leaking out, for example, or where confidence is being buried under threats, guilt, and fear.

So, let's get to work. As we move onto the next bend in the road, let's return to the image of our garden.

A BEND IN THE ROAD

IDENTIFYING THREATS
AND AREAS OF WEAKNESS

Let's begin with a careful walk-about in our gardens. Revisit your truths and untruths. Then think about potential threats to the healthful environment you want to create for yourself. As always, be gentle, yet honest. Your goal right now is just to identify areas where you might need protection. The actual protection will come later. That will be another part of the journey. This first assignment is challenging enough.

To identify threats to your well-being, ask yourself the questions below and attempt to give honest and thoughtful answers. Be open about your fears and your uneasiness. Identify your weak areas so that, later, you can build protection around them.

As you go through the questions, it will be important to voice *all* of the threats you feel—whether real or simply perceived—because all are influencing the way you live your life. Some of the threats to your sense of well-being might surprise you. They might come from unlikely places, even places you thought were safe or trustworthy. Do not talk yourself out of the uneasy feelings that come. Honestly identify the threats. You need to bring them to light or they will continue to lurk in the shadows, causing you distress with no way toward resolution.

The following questions will help you inspect your garden. As you consider the questions, threats and weak areas will reveal themselves. Write them down in the space after each question or in the margins.

What threatens you?

What triggers the desire to run, to hide, to stand paralyzed?

What causes your body and spirit to prepare to fight?

Where is trauma encroaching on your ability to live in peace?

Who or what makes you uneasy?

How is suffering affecting your daily activities?

How is suffering affecting your future plans?

Where and when do you feel your courage leaking?

What is burying your confidence, your strength?

What are the threats to your healing?

Where is trauma encroaching on your ability to live in peace?

What effects do you feel in your body? In your spirit? In your emotions?

Where do you need protection?

Now divvy them up between the two garden images that follow.

Image #1: The first image allows you to identify intruders that are threatening to come *into* your garden. Write on the arrows coming in from the outside: identify the dangers, threats, and untruths that you feel want to intrude on your place of well-being. Add more arrows as needed.

Image #2: The second image allows you to identify the positive influences that you feel are at risk of slipping away. Write on the arrows going out from the inside: identify the beauty, good, and truth that are in jeopardy of slipping away. Add more arrows as needed.

You may need to come back to this bend in the road often. As you go through the days, and even weeks or months, of your journey, you will likely recognize threats that you did not see before. Whenever you become aware of a new threat or area of weakness, name it on your page. *This is a profound step in moving forward.*

As you do, perhaps it would be good to speak these words:

"These threats are forceful and manipulative. If my garden is to grow strong and healthy, *protection is definitely needed.*"

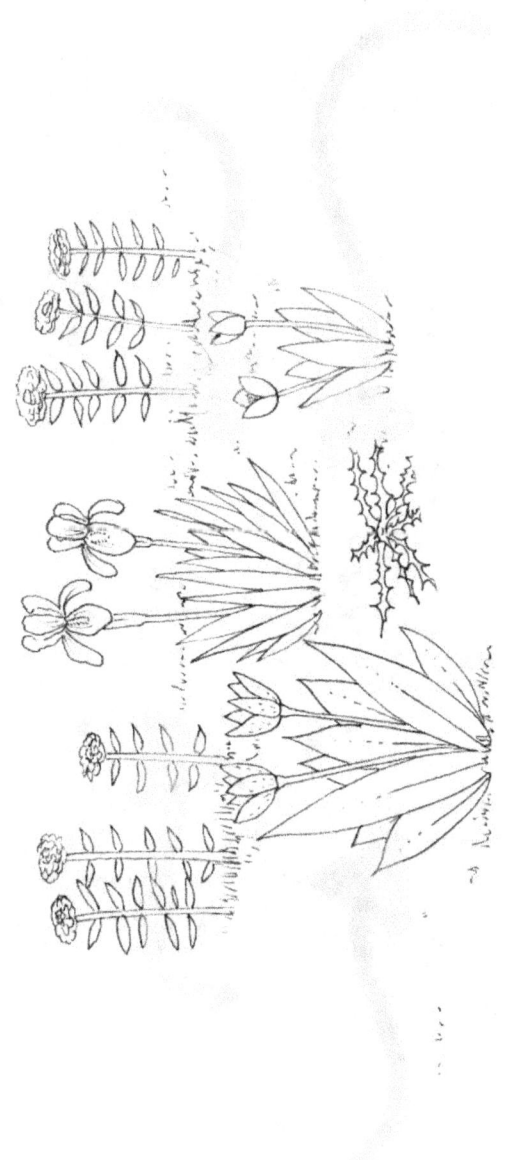

283

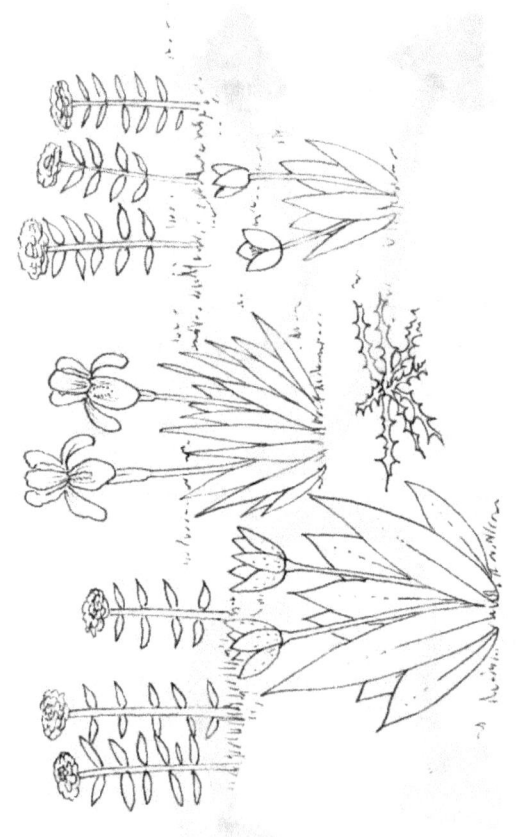

65

SETTING BOUNDARIES

We now clearly see that, if our garden is to grow in beauty and truth, it will need protection. We can create this protection by setting up boundaries.

So, what do we mean by boundaries? What does this look like in our lives? Boundaries have two purposes: to keep harmful influences out and to keep good in. Some boundaries are as simple and straightforward as what time we go to bed, what types of movies we watch, what foods we eat, or who we spend time with. They might also include how much time we spend doing certain activities, like being alone, sitting on the computer, or thinking about the past.

In fact, as I mentioned briefly in the previous section, whether you knew it or not, we have been setting boundaries all along our journey:

- We have talked about the ability to look at portions of our suffering for limited amounts of time. This is a boundary. It protects us from being swept away by the intensity of the pain.

- We have talked about intentionally seeing the good in our lives. This is a boundary. It keeps suffering from taking over all parts of our lives.

- We have looked at the actual event of our suffering and discovered its beginning and end. This is a boundary. It keeps the event in a particular timeframe and protects us from constant illogical fear.

You have been doing good work, and you likely already feel the effects of these boundaries that you are putting into place. Yet, there is more we can do.

We can use boundaries, for example, to help with our triggers—those places, people, events, or sensory inputs that we connect to our suffering and can set off powerful emotional and behavioral responses whenever we encounter them. These triggers can come up unexpectedly and in common, everyday situations; a sound, an experience, even a "look" from someone can pull us suddenly and definitively back into our time of suffering. So, establishing boundaries for certain places, events, and even people that we know will act as triggers may be particularly necessary in the early days of our healing.

But what boundaries should we put around our gardens of truth and untruth? And how do we go about building those boundaries? There are three specific types of boundaries that we would do well to consider; however, first, since we have a tendency to go to extremes—either giving open rein to whatever comes our way or building walls that shut us up in fear-binding seclusion—let's look at a few boundary-setting tips:

- Set your boundary with truth. The structure of the boundary must be truth that can stand against the lies that trauma whispers in your ear.

- Set your boundary in reality. Wishful thinking does not make a good boundary and is easily pushed aside by the intensity of trauma.

- Set your boundary with intentionality. Casual good ideas, other people's suggestions, trendy philosophies—these will all bend to trauma's purposeful attempts to control. So, you must be intentional, determined, and deliberate as you move forward.

Now, let's consider three types of boundaries we should be aware of and learn how to observe ourselves to decide whether we need these boundaries around our gardens.

BOUNDARIES ON OUR MIND TIME AND EMOTIONS

Mind time and emotional strength—we have a limited quantity of both. When our mind time (the time spent in conscious thought) is depleted, we feel stressed. When our emotions are depleted, we feel exhausted.

So, how can we spend these precious resources wisely?

By making two observations of ourselves, we can determine if we need boundaries in these areas.

Observation 1: How much of my mind time per day is filled with the suffering? In other words, how much time do I spend each day thinking about it—having pretend conversations, dwelling on the what-ifs, pondering the details, and playing out scenarios in my mind? Do I feel emotionally exhausted? How many of my decisions include the suffering as a large part of the reasoning process? Is my suffering in the forefront of my thoughts? Is it draining my emotions?

But I need to think about it, you might respond. *It is important for me to process.*

Remember, *trauma consumes.* It will always demand more time in our minds and more emotional expenditure. If we follow the natural path, we will find ourselves stressed and emotionally exhausted.

Observation 2: How many of my conversations with others come back around to the suffering? Can I converse with others without bringing "it" to attention? When I am asked about myself, is "it" the first thing I want to tell? When someone else shares a painful experience, do I feel the need to share my story? These can be signals that the trauma is becoming our identity.

In the beginning, it is natural for the topic to be consuming. But a large part of our journey has been learning to express our suffering—to get to a place where we are no longer trying to hide it and no longer shamed by it. Once we get to that point, and we become more comfortable speaking with others about our suffering, we usually discover further evidence of healing: we can have conversations that do not include and do not even refer to the event or the trauma. This does not happen because of fear or shame, but because the suffering is loosening its grip on us. It is not consuming us as it once did.

In these later stages of our journey, healthy expression of suffering at appropriate times is good; however, a consuming need to think and talk about the suffering can be unhealthy.

BOUNDARIES ON OUR COPING BEHAVIORS AND ADDICTIVE RESPONSES

My coping behaviors were watching HGTV and shopping the clearance racks. When my mind could not cope with reality, I would escape, watching programs that "fixed" things and sleuthing a good bargain. Later, a dear friend helped me purge my closet of the items I had accumulated in sizes too large for me—yes, it seems hiding in larger-than-necessary clothing had become another coping behavior. We all have things that we do to help us through difficult times. This can be healthy. However, these ways of coping can easily begin to consume more and more. When they do, the habit of escape can then become a detriment, leading us into a place of numbness and even addiction. So, we need to observe these behaviors in ourselves honestly for any signs that boundaries are needed.

Observation 1: How often and how quickly do I return to a behavior of escape? Am I spending more time hiding and escaping than actually living in the real world?

Observation 2: Is my way of coping taking me toward a greater sense of well-being? Or is it beginning to cause harm to my health, body, mind, relationships, or emotions?

BOUNDARIES ON OUR RELATIONSHIPS

Some part of your suffering may be connected to a relationship. The list of potential relational scenarios that cause suffering seems endless, along with the needed boundaries for those scenarios. So, let's start by reminding ourselves that our boundaries must be realistic. We cannot build boundaries that will protect us from *all* hurt and negative interactions. We cannot run from *all* confrontation.

For this discussion, then, we are focusing on those relationships that are directly related to our trauma. Having protection in those relationships is necessary if we are to move forward and not remain mired in the conflict.

In particular, there is a real and healthy place for boundaries in the following types of relationships:

- Relationships that are a strong trigger for unhealthy responses, including panic.
- Relationships in which abuse, negative influence, and manipulation still continue.

For these relationships, clear boundaries are a necessary part of our healing. The types of boundaries needed will vary depending on the details of each relationship; they will also vary in their degree of severity.

A boundary of interaction, for example, might include:
- Being careful in the frequency or depth of conversations and joint activities with another

Likewise, a boundary in communication might vary in its severity:
- Allowing voice contact but nothing in-person
- Allowing in-person contact but not texting—or the reverse
- Not allowing voice contact at all

Some boundaries might be temporary, while others will be permanent. The severity and extent of a boundary can also be adjusted based on the other person's response. Say the other person respects your boundary; in that case, you might choose to make the boundary less severe after time. If the other person pushes back, however, you can adjust the boundary to become stronger.

What about kindness, love, and grace? you may ask. Kindness, love, and grace are necessary in our relationships. However, it is possible to be kind and to show love and grace—and still set boundaries.

The truth that I want you to hear is that you have permission to set boundaries in many types of relationships for your good and for the good of others. Clear boundaries actually plant the seed for peaceful interactions.

As we grow stronger in our healing and peace with the way life is now, we also may grow stronger in our ability to welcome a new kind of relationship with those connected to our story. We don't want to miss out on reclaimed relationships if that door opens in a healthy way. A clear boundary in one area may clear the pathway to interaction in another.

We cannot shut ourselves off from all potential hurt or misunderstanding. And we do not want to feed bitterness or revenge. However, we do have permission to set boundaries that protect us and our families on an already difficult path of healing. In particular, ongoing abuse always calls for clear boundaries. We care for ourselves by observing for any signs that boundaries are needed.

Observation 1: Am I engaged in relationships that are a source of ongoing abuse?

Observation 2: Do I experience trauma-related symptoms that are detrimental to my well-being in some situations?

PARENTAL AND OTHER FAMILY RELATIONSHIPS

What about relationships with our parents? Do we not have instructions to honor and respect parents in all things? As adult children, we learn that to honor, to respect, is not the same as "to remain under the control of." Yes, we honor. Yes, we respect. But, sin and suffering impact how that dialogue is expressed.

How do we honor abusive parents?

- We honor them by not returning the abuse they gave (or give) to us.
- We honor them by not enabling their bad behavior, nor allowing them to continue their abusive ways with us, or others under our protection.
- We honor them by giving them clear boundaries and consequences when they are not repentant nor willing to work toward ending their abusive ways.

When a family member becomes the perpetrator, the abuser, the source of the danger, he/she gives up the anticipated or expected relationship in the family. The closeness of trust and intimacy is not given "on demand." Nor is it owed simply because of a family title.

We do honor the position of parent:

- by *not* continuing that abuse with our own children.
- by careful protection from those relationships that attempt to continue the abuse to the next generation.
- by stopping the cycle.

If generational suffering is to subside, move out of prominence in the story . . . then one generation must set strong and powerful boundaries . . . with kindness and respect.

Perhaps your mind is reeling. Where do I need boundaries? Where do they need to be firm and strong and where do I leave open a small gate? How do I do this with wisdom and not with fear or over-reaction? We may need much time at this bend in the road.

You will discover the boundaries that are necessary for you. Sometimes, we are made aware of a necessary boundary because we find ourselves in a bad situation . . . that "I wish I had not" moment. This is a good time to note the potential need for a boundary in that situation. Watch for it again.

Our boundaries are not intended to keep us from all pain or discomfort. That would be wishful thinking! The boundaries are meant to protect from the attacks that will overwhelm us or take us to a point of despair. Some onslaughts will get past, and we will feel them deeply. However, even then, we have permission to set a boundary of how much and how long we will indulge that particular experience of pain.

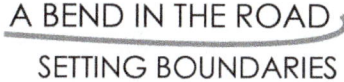 

A BEND IN THE ROAD
SETTING BOUNDARIES

Begin the process of defining your specific boundaries. Begin a list in the area around your garden. Then, write the boundaries you are sure about on the fence slats.

In the days and weeks that follow, continue to watch for those moments when the need for a boundary is clear—and set it with confidence. Come back to this page and write it on one of the fence slats.

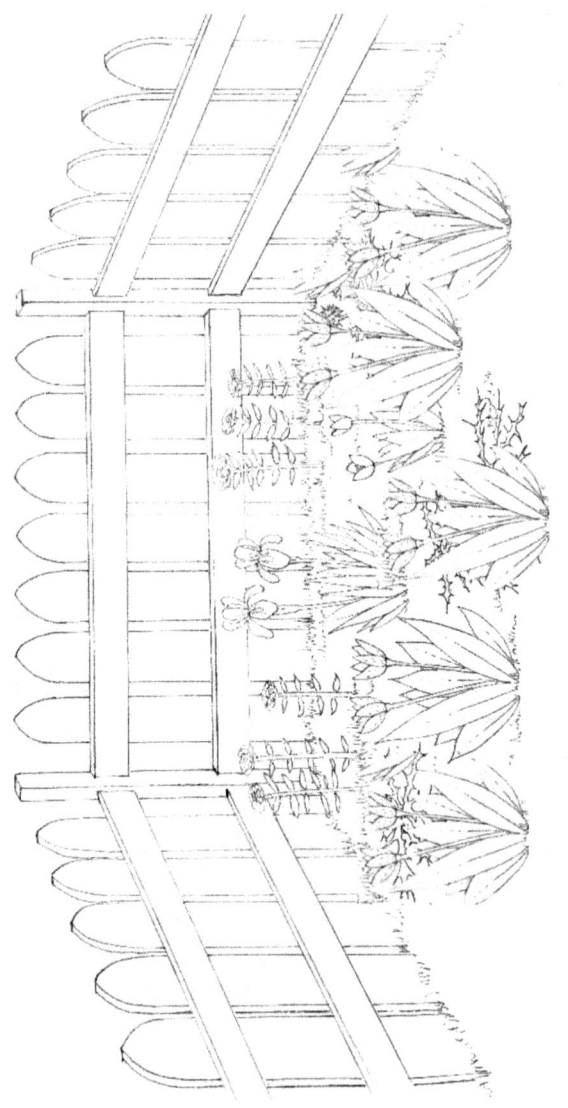

292

THE CHALLENGE OF CHANGE

*It is sometimes necessary
to revisit some part
of the journey in order to
reorganize, redesign, or refashion
before moving forward.*

Perhaps, you have noticed that I encourage you to "talk to yourself" along this journey. The truth is, we already have these internal conversations, so we may as well learn how to talk to ourselves in ways that are wise and *for our good*. One way we can do this is to change our vocabulary.

At various bends in the road, we have faced hard conversations and new challenges, and during these times, whether you realized it or not, we deliberately began to adjust the way we spoke to ourselves, changing our vocabulary . . .

from untruth to truth,

from fear to courage, and

from despair to hope.

It had to happen. Because if it didn't, we would continue speaking to ourselves in the same way we have over the past months or even years— in a way that leads us deeper into the despair and control of our suffering.

You see, our very own words have been adding to the destruction. Our conversations with ourselves have fed the pain that began with the crisis moment and then eventually integrated into every part of our lives. These words and conversations sound something like this:

All is lost.

Nothing good ever happens to me.

I am to blame.

I can never trust anyone again.

I can't get this out of my mind.

I am not valuable to anyone.

Why me?

No one understands.

This is who I am; nothing good can come of it. How can I fix this?

I always make wrong choices.

Do any of these sound familiar?

I take this opportunity to remind you of the courageous work you are doing on this journey. *Nothing will ever change?* That is no longer true. Changes have settled into your thinking process already. Some are subtle, and some are monumental—but all are profound in your journey of healing.

So, as you think about the past,

    as despair challenges hope,

        as untruth whispers in your ear,

            as illogical fear disturbs your peace,

                as suffering points to your place in the script,

    you must speak new words to yourself.

The upcoming bend in the road is an opportunity to *see the changes* that have happened inside of you. It is not a test. There is nothing to achieve or to prove to anyone. However, this exercise is necessary, because we have grown so accustomed to seeing the negative that we tend to be blind to the positive changes. The pressing difficulties and lingering pain are so quick to claim center stage that sometimes we even feel *guilty* drawing attention to positive moments in our lives. No more.

In the following bend, we will declare a conquest over those words that, for so long, have threatened to defeat us. No adjustment is too small. No transformation is too trivial.

No whisper of truth is insignificant.

A BEND IN THE ROAD,
A NEW VOCABULARY

You are growing in companionship with yourself as you journey through healing. Take notice. And if there is vocabulary to be corrected, now is the time to confront it.

First, take some time to discover shifts that have already happened in how you communicate with yourself—in how you encourage and discourage, speak truth and correct untruth. Look back through the previous chapters to help you remember how you were speaking to yourself and compare that with how you are speaking to yourself now.

As you look back, consider how you have improved your vocabulary as a traveling companion. Then write down your thoughts on paper.

It might help to revisit the damaging statements below and then add your own:

All is lost.

Nothing good ever happens to me.

I am to blame.

I can never trust anyone again.

I can't get this out of my mind.

I am not valuable to anyone.

Why me?

No one understands.

This is who I am; nothing good can come of it. How can I fix this?

I always make wrong choices.

Do any of these destructive statements capture beliefs that you once held about yourself or your life but that have changed? This is the time to speak honestly, without pretense.

Write your damaging words on the page so they become real to you. It's the hidden poison that does the most damage.

Then below the damaging words, write down the more constructive, truthful statements that you have started to believe and speak to yourself instead.

When you are finished, move onto the next exercise.

While doing the previous exercise, it is possible that you became aware of some negative self-talk that *still* haunts you. This is the time to bring those words to light. Write them down on the next page and take note of the untruth that they carry. Notice the harm they inflict.

Now think about how you could change those words so that they lead . . .

away from untruth and toward truth,

away from fear and toward courage, and

away from despair and toward hope.

As an example, a dear mentor taught me a valuable lesson that I have applied many times in conversations both with others and with myself. He taught me to create a phrase that I could use repeatedly as my response when faced with negative conversations.

Let's say someone asks me for more details than I want to share. My response phrase could be, "I have nothing more to say about that." If the person asks again or even comes at it from another angle, I can simply repeat it: "I have nothing more to say about that." I can say it calmly, with no added dialogue. And as my mentor told me, I've never had to repeat it past the third time.

We can do this in conversation with ourselves, as well: Susan, what a mess you make of everything.

"God says I am valuable to Him."

Did you see what you just did? That was stupid.

"God says I am valuable to Him."

Don't think anyone really loves you.

"God says I am valuable to Him."

It works.

Create your own small responses—two words, a phrase, whatever . . . just be sure it is truth—and write them down in the space below. Then practice them and remember to repeat them when negative self-talk threatens. You may need to practice often. But I assure you that after time, truth always wins.

THE REALITY OF FEAR
AND THE ASSURANCE THAT HOLDS US

Fearful: it is not a word I would have used to describe myself.

Until . . . everything familiar was shattered. I found myself pulled, without warning, into a reality where constant undeniable truth destroyed any sense of safety. Around every corner, there was another unimaginable revelation. Looking back at me in the mirror was a woman I did not recognize, standing in a terrifying and accusatory world.

And suddenly, *fearful* was a dominant descriptive. Permeating everything.

Aggressive. Destructive. Palpable.

At times, fear would grasp with such suddenness and strength that I would find myself on the floor, breathless, unable to reason. Literally afraid to live forward into the next few minutes.

In those moments, our options for assistance narrow dramatically. For me, there was only one option. I literally crawled to the only One whom I could imagine offering a lifeline. I needed a simple message of survival. And He replied in a few paraphrased words from Proverbs 3:25–26. The message He gave to me was simply:

Do not give in to sudden fear . . . the LORD is at your side.

I printed that message on paper and put it on my refrigerator. I ran to it often and held it in my hands. I repeated it over and over in those moments:

"Do not give in to sudden fear."

"Do not give in to sudden fear."

"Do not give in to sudden fear."

"The LORD is at your side."

I still have that paper, tucked in a journal as a remembrance. It held life. It held protection. It held onto me. It was one of my tethers, a reminder of God's presence and love.

Fear sometimes assaults us like this, pressing down, instantly taking our breath away. But sometimes, it is more stealthy. It seeps into the soil of our life garden, almost unrecognizable, until we become aware that our choices and our perspective are tainted by the anxiety and dread that we have absorbed, polluted by the event that planted the fear.

As I write this chapter, I am sitting with my leg elevated, in a cast. I recently had surgery to repair bones broken in a fall. At the time of the accident, there was no critical moment of fear. I tripped (on boots I had left in my own path), went down, and the bones broke. No time for fear. My experience of surgery and recovery so far has been fairly peaceful. I have not had a lot of pain. I am mobile, rolling about on a knee scooter.

This experience did not come with any great, sudden assault of fear. Yet, over time, I became aware that my thoughts about the future were colored by anxiety related to the event. What if other bones give way? What if I am just walking along and fall? What about stairs? What about my travels—what if I break a bone on a trip? Will I ever feel safe running again? My bones are not strong. What if other parts of my body are not strong? What if I can't trust my body?

Fear. Quiet anxiety and doubt clouded my outlook.

This type of fear is dangerous. It hinders our emotional healing and turns our focus away from possibility and toward uncertainty and our own vulnerability.

Fear. A distressing emotion aroused by impending danger, evil, pain.

The thing is, fear is often a reasonable response. There is reason for fear. Suffering often comes as a result of something unknown becoming known, something unexpected being revealed, something perceived as safe becoming dangerous. So we have uncertainty. *If one unimaginable thing is now reality*, we wonder, *then what else is in question?* It's as if we're walking around on a moonless night—there is no way to see what is in front of us, to say nothing of what is behind us and on every side. And we respond to this uncertainty with fear.

Fear is real. In many situations, we cannot *not fear*. Fear just comes, and the reality is that we must be talked out of it. But who can do that? Who can speak words that are trustworthy and full of power? Words that, when spoken, actually impart peace and calm? Who can overwhelm the fear that overwhelms us?

> "The LORD is at your side."

God used those few words to talk me out of the aggressive, destructive, palpable moments of fear. It wasn't instant, however, and took work. I would speak the words, *"Do not give in to fear"* over and over again, sometimes without a breath between and sometimes whispered; sometimes I used the words as a shield, to block fear's arrows, and sometimes I shot them out like arrows into the spiritual darkness around me.

> "The LORD is at your side."

Then after several minutes, calm would come. The assault was over for the moment. But it wasn't because of the words themselves. It's not as if the words hold some kind of magic. Rather, the fear was overwhelmed and subdued by the presence of the LORD *with me.* It is the One who stands with us who imparts the strength we so desperately need; the words simply act as a tether to hold our focus on Him in the moment.

Have you felt fear? Do you know the way it washes over you, taking your breath away, clouding your reason? Is your view of the future polluted by anxiety and doubt that grow out of the fear that has been planted?

The LORD is at your side.

Our fear is not a surprise to our perfect Traveling Companion. In fact, this reality of fear is the foundation for one of I AM's most frequent promises to us:

> *I know you are feeling fear . . . hold onto this truth:* I AM *with you.*

Our God tethers us to Himself with profound words that speak powerful reality. Let's look at and think about some of these words:

- For I am the LORD your God who takes hold of your right hand and says to you, Do not fear; I will help you. (Isaiah 41:13)

Many assurances are hollow. Many promises have been broken. But not this one: "It is I," He says. "I hold your hand." This assurance, this promise, this tether to God's presence is strong, because it comes from the LORD, who knows no fear. Everything and everyone answers to His call. Nothing can overwhelm Him. There are no unknowns for Him, no uncertainty. And yet He chooses to be by your side, saying, "It is I."

- So do not fear, for I am with you; do not be dismayed, for I am your God. I will strengthen you and help you; I will uphold you with my righteous right hand. (Isaiah 41:10)

Before your moment of fear, God promised His presence. Before you felt your anxiety, He reached out to uphold you. Before the suffering was known to you, He was your God.

He knows. He sees. He feels. He hears. He is stronger than any threat that causes the fear. He strengthens you and protects you from sinking to that place from which you cannot rise.

- You came near when I called you, and you said, "Do not fear." (Lamentations 3:57)

He is near. He is present. He hears your call and responds with assurance, saying to you, "Do not give in to fear."

- God is our refuge and strength, an ever-present help in trouble. Therefore we will not fear, though the earth give way and the mountains fall into the heart of the sea, though its waters roar and foam and the mountains quake with their surging. (Psalm 46:1–3)

During real fear-inspiring events, there is a refuge. In those times of debilitating weakness, there is One from whom you can draw strength. God is present with you. You can seek His refuge and experience release from fear. When all else gives way . . . you have a safe place.

What can I say to you in the midst of your paralyzing fear?

- Say to those with fearful hearts, "Be strong, do not fear." (Isaiah 35:4).

There were times, in the presence of oppressive fear, that my face was gray, my eyes shadowed, my countenance downcast. The fear expressed itself through my physical being. But I discovered that whenever I turn my face to the LORD, my God, and grasp the tether that holds me to Him, the fear releases its powerful grasp—and in that release, a new expression flows from me.

- I sought the LORD, and he answered me; he delivered me from all my fears. Those who look to him are radiant; their faces are never covered with shame. (Psalm 34:4–5)

Radiance? Amid aggressive, destructive, palpable fear? Inexplicable, but true. The presence of the LORD shines through our countenance, replacing the gray desperation of fear with brightness. The dependable promise of His place at our side breaks through any outward expression of fear and shame.

Fear is a reality.

But, in that fear, God holds us with the assurance of His presence and His goodness. These are our tethers: *It is I. I hold your hand.*

By Him, we are delivered from the stronghold of fear.

And from Him, our radiance becomes a reality.

What truth is He holding out to you? What assurance tethers you to Him? What message from Him will you write and memorize and use as a shield? What will you speak, as arrows, into the uncertainty that surrounds you?

What truth will shine through you? What radiance?

68. RE-

Consider the prefix *re-*.

Together, these two letters carry a powerful definition: "to do again." It carries with it an implication of *going back* to something, not necessarily to duplicate what you did before but to change or improve upon it—*to do something anew*.

When we decide to *re*decorate a room, for example, we probably have no intention of painting the same color on the walls, using the same fabrics, and hanging the same pictures in the same locations. No! Instead, we intend to decorate the room anew—to give the room new life by making changes and improvements.

Throughout our journey, we have carefully and gently taken on several tasks of *re-*. With each bend in the road, we have been challenged to *go back* (to *re*member or *re*visit something in our past) and then to move forward again (to *re*sume our journey) with some sort of change or improvement—*to do things in a new way.*

- We have *re*organized our timeline of events, discovering a beginning and an end to the crisis event.

- We have *re*organized our priorities, removing suffering from its place of demand and control.

- We have *re*designed the way we look at our lives, giving suffering its true place yet also bringing blessings and provisions into the picture.

- We have *re*fashioned our emotional responses: mourning loss rather than attempting to replace it, expressing fear rather than running from it, looking at pain rather than hiding it.

- We have *re*claimed memories, songs, seasons, experiences that were once connected with only pain.

Do you see it? Have you felt it?

In my own journey of healing, as I was writing this very chapter, I had the experience of personally connecting with this concept of *re-*, or this concept of *going back and then moving forward in a new way*. I had just started writing the chapter and was happy with the main idea—it was positive and hopeful. I put in a good day of writing, but when I was done, I saved the chapter in the "in progress" file, because I didn't feel like it was quite complete. *No worries, though.* I thought. *The rest would come.*

And then later that same day, I hit an emotional wall. From out of nowhere, I was extremely overwhelmed by a sense of failure in a particular area of my healing. This failure was not related to the cause of my crisis moment but had to do with one of the responses I'd held since that time. I was inconsolable. I was angry with myself, accusing, weeping. My exact words were, "It's all ruined. It cannot be undone. It's hopeless."

My Traveling Companion, my perfect Good Shepherd, allowed me to sit on the path for a time, and then He simply and quietly spoke, saying, *"This is the time for re-."*

What?! This is the time for re-?

I slowly realized that He wanted me to hear the words that He had just given earlier in the day. Yes, He had allowed me to feel this "palpable need for change" for a reason. But that reason was not so that I would take up the burden of failure or despair. It was so that I would *revisit* the issue, which would enable me *to move forward in a new way.*

Suddenly the profoundness of His earlier message came to life.

A new awareness had come to me about a particular response to suffering. And what had I done? I had turned it onto myself as accusation. Assigning shame. Pronouncing judgment. How often had I done this on my journey?

> How often do we see some piece of our story in a new light and respond by immediately and willingly taking on the burden and accusation of failure—when what is really intended is simply re-?

In those moments of unbridled despair, my focus was on my assumed failure, when what I really should have been focused on was gratitude for the wisdom and courage I would gain on a new path.

"Susan, I did not bring this to your attention to accuse you," I heard my companion say. *"I just wanted you to see this so you can do it differently from this point forward."*

It is not always easy to *go back* just so that we can move forward *in a new way*. But *it is possible*. It is also possible to sit on the path and refuse to budge, more ready to stay in despair than to accept our companion's opening toward healing.

Which will you choose?

The simple fact that you have made it this far suggests that you are ready to continue to choose *re-*. In fact, our whole journey has been centered on this idea. On our very first steps, we went back to the crisis. From there, we continually moved forward, fully aware of the suffering, yet introducing hope, leaning into peace, and reclaiming joy. And at nearly every bend in the road, we have chosen *re-*.

The next bend will be no different.

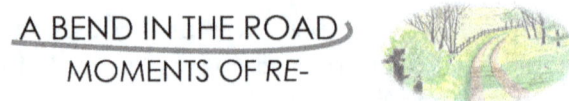
Is there any area on your journey that has been calling you to quiet contemplation? Is it necessary to revisit some part of your journey in order to reorganize, redesign, or reclaim so that you can move forward?

You don't need to think of everything. That will only discourage you. Just think of *something*. That will encourage.

If you find yourself inclined to respond in extremes—either to overwhelm yourself and make impossible demands, or stand gazing into the night sky as if this does not concern you at all—it would be best to check with your loving travel companion. You can trust him to reveal the truth . . . but only enough for this moment of time and only for the purpose of healing.

It might also help to think carefully about what needs gentle, but intentional, attention in each of the following areas. Then write down your ideas.

Reorganize.   Redesign.   Reclaim.

Those moments. Those "screaming in the car" moments.

I committed to be honest with you. This means that, sometimes, I am gentle and encouraging; other times, I give warnings; and at this time, I am being a bit raw and maybe even unsavory.

But the truth is, the car seems to be my safe place for releasing emotion. Fierce, unbridled, graphic emotion.

During several traumatic events I experienced, my car, while it was moving down the road, was the one place I could scream and not fear that someone would stare, run, or call the police! It was the one place where I could . . .

> shout my accusations,
>> sob with inhibition,
>>> and literally express my pain with abandon.

Things are different now, though. I have purpose in my life, along with hope, peace, and joy. I am even helping others walk through their journeys of pain. Those "screaming in the car" moments are years in the past. Or so I thought.

Until just yesterday, I found myself screaming in the car. No, really—ugly-face screaming.

I cannot even remember what triggered my emotion. But suddenly, I was there again, in the depth of my pain. I felt the bitterness of betrayal, the shame of my naive trust, the lies of others, and my own bad choices.

I could not contain it. And I was screaming. In the car. At 4:00 in the afternoon.

I tell you this because I don't want you to be alarmed when it happens to you. I don't want you to feel disappointment and failure.

I don't know where or when, but it will happen. Maybe you won't scream. Maybe, instead, you will sit paralyzed in a chair. Or maybe you will need to escape from the aisles of a store because you feel like you can't breathe. Yes, I know that feeling too.

However it surfaces, don't be afraid. It is one more layer of awareness. And *you will survive.*

You see, you cannot possibly experience all layers of pain at once. This would bury you or destroy you. And so, the layers peel back one or two at a time, little bits of understanding rising in your consciousness. Uninvited. Unexpected.

So, what do we do when this happens?

> We get to a safe place.
> We give ourselves time for the experience.
> We express. We offload. We *feel.*
> We reach out to someone we trust and say, "Hang on to me."

I will tell you what most often happens to me: Even though the wound has reopened and looks disgusting, spewing abhorrent evidence of suffering all around, the pain does not go to the desperate and destructive place that it did in the beginning. My precious Traveling Companion, I Am, does not allow it. It is as if He establishes a boundary, saying, "Here—and no further. There is no need to go to that darkest place again." And when the momentary storm settles, I find that another portion of bitterness, fear, and evil has been swept away. When will it emerge again? I don't know. But for now, it is calm.

How did it invade my peace?

>Protective veil ripped away, my eyes unable to avert from
the visual, the sound, the emotion (why with such clarity?),
loss and betrayal rushing into my soul without warning.

For a terrifying moment, the trauma invades my calm.

>The open wound calls me to despair, releasing pain,
releasing parts of me that
stun me, frighten me.

Yet, *releasing.*

>Cleansing.
>Purging.
>Purifying.

Valuable.

>My pain is valuable.
>I let it flow over me and around me and past me
and . . . *away.*

With determination, I hold unswervingly to the hope that anchors me—

>my only Faithful One.
>Jesus, my Good Shepherd,
>God, my Protector.

And as I lift

>my broken heart,
>my weary soul,
>my fractured pride to Him,

He reaches out to lovingly bind up my wounds.

Those moments.

>They will come.
>You will survive.
>You will grow stronger.

What a journey we are on! Even this far along the path, we are discovering that we can still move in and out of emotions. We might be sailing along with our heads held high and then suddenly, we are in a puddle of tears.

We have known from the beginning that coming to peace would not be a straight road. We determined that this journey would require contemplation and intention. But it is the road we have chosen, the one we committed to move forward on anyway—and we are!

As with many other parts of the road, however, moving forward on this chosen path often means letting go of incorrect expectations and unrealistic demands. We have done this at various points along our journey. For example, we . . .

- have not tried to forget the event,
- have accepted that all relationships cannot be restored, and
- have not attempted to put life back together the way it was—or to create a new life that does not include an awareness of the past.

Now we are at a place where we must understand . . .

- that there may still be tears to be shed, emotions to be expressed; and
- that just because we have started down a good path of healing does not mean we can assume it will always be that way.

This is the reality of our journey—of my journey. I like to think that I am directionally correct most of the time. But the reality is there are still "those moments." There are still those days that bring memories, triggers, emotions, difficult decisions, and dare I say it—even *new* events of suffering. New fears. New pain.

When these moments arise, it helps to pause and look around for a while. By doing so, we can both see where we are now and reflect on where we have been during important points along our journey.

This is a good time to stop for a bend in the road that will help us to do just that.

A BEND IN THE ROAD
ALONG THE WAY

Below you will find a set of cards with images of figures. We will use these little figures to help us understand and express our *emotional states and perspectives*, both now and along the way. This visual task is meant to help us honestly "see ourselves," both where we are and where we have been on our journey, to ensure that we don't get stuck and that we keep moving in the right direction.

I encourage you to cut the cards apart and then to hold each card in your hand for a time, studying the figure. (You might prefer to make a copy of the page and cut them apart.) Pay careful attention to the direction of the gaze and the posture of the body. Likely, you have experienced some, if not all, of these postures. Do you "see" yourself in a particular figure or figures? There is something powerful about holding these images in your hands and connecting your own experiences to them visually. I think of them as our little friends who can help us tell our story.

Use your observations about these figures to have a conversation with yourself.

First, think about the crisis event and your time of suffering—when it began, how it progressed, and so on. Use the figures to tell the story of your emotions and perspectives. Perhaps you could line them up to synchronize with your timeline of suffering. Or maybe you could label them with certain events you've written down in your bends in the road. If your journey is anything like mine, you will have experienced most of the emotions displayed by these figures more than once.

As you reflect back, clearly note any of "those moments." Do you repeatedly go back to a certain issue? At what times did you stall and turn back, with your face to the crisis and your back to the future once more? How long did you stay there? Did you turn things around to face the future again, or are you perhaps still stuck in that place?

Next, use the figures to discover where you are right now. Are you still looking back? Are you directionally forward but you have your head down? Are you in a heap on the floor?

Take some time with these sweet little friends and return to them periodically to check on your progress. You might do this whenever you have one of "those" moments" or just when you sense that you may be stuck or headed in the wrong direction. Or you might choose to set a regular "check-in" routine on your calendar.

If you find that you are "down" for an extended period of time, attention is needed. What is happening in your life that would trigger this response? If necessary, reach out to someone you trust.

Whenever you see that you are at least directionally correct—for example, facing to the right (the future), even if your head is down—you will know that you are beginning to take back control, attempting to move forward.

There is something therapeutically helpful in seeing your mental and emotional states in this simple way: it helps you see the possibilities.

And *that* is an important, monumental bend in your journey.

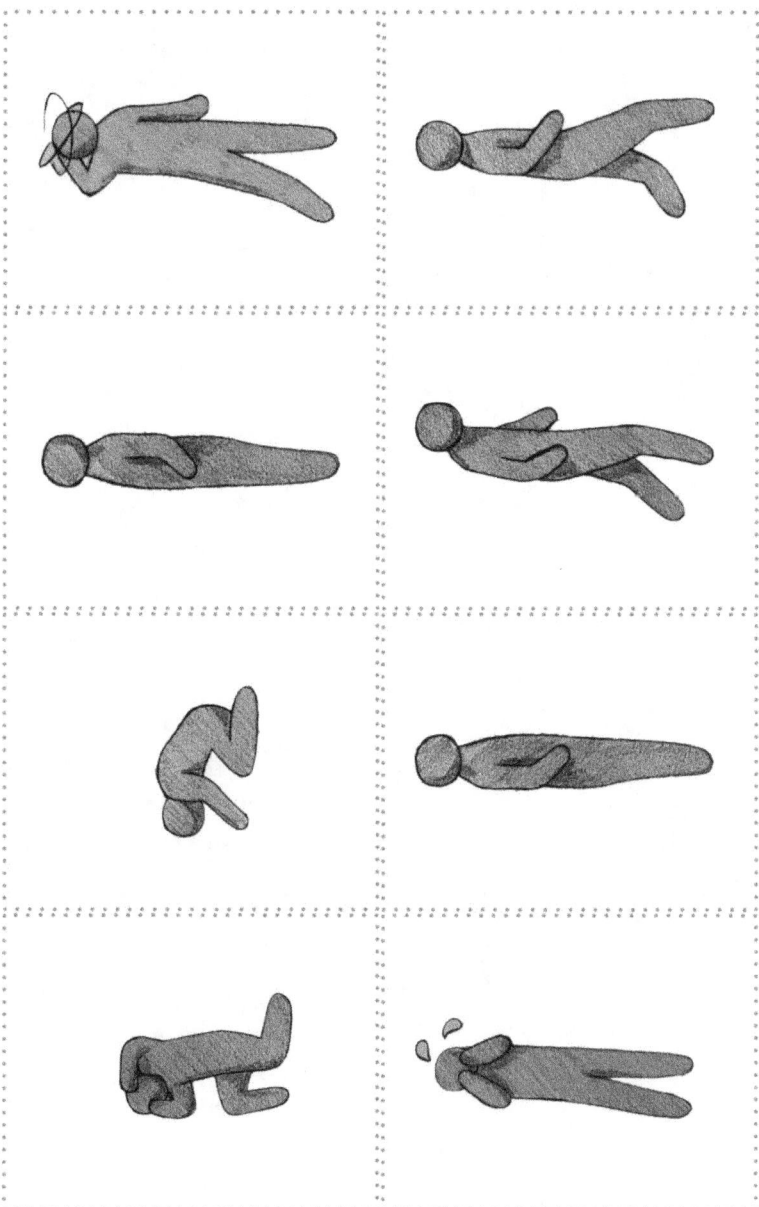

MOVING FORWARD

*The ground beneath you has been
shaky, uncertain, even dangerous.
Perhaps, as you gain your footing,
your eyes are beginning to lift,
even momentarily,
to see beyond the next step.*

72
BEYOND THE NEXT STEP

Did you ever learn to roller skate? If so, maybe your experience was a bit like mine. I remember my eyes being glued to the floor—and to my feet. I was attempting to *see* the next step, virtually willing my foot to lift and then to quickly connect with the floor again. All the while, I was anticipating, with panic, that moment when one foot was in the air and the other was on *moving ground*. Nothing about the process felt safe.

Eyes on the floor, eyes on my feet, foot lifts, body moves forward; eyes on the floor, eyes on my feet, other foot lifts, body moves forward.

I was amazed at the people who sailed past me, eyes up, looking ahead, scanning the faces across the rink, greeting and interacting with others. How did they do it all at once? How did they manage to skate without looking at their feet? How did they smile and wave at others as the ground continually moved beneath them?

Eyes on the floor, eyes on my feet, foot lifts, body moves forward; repeat.

I had similar thoughts when attempting to move forward during the powerful onslaught of suffering. *Eyes directly in front of me, eyes on my feet, take one step; repeat.* All the while, I was on the verge of panic, as the ground seemed to shift with uncertainty beneath me.

Subconsciously, I was aware of others who seemed to sail past me, looking ahead at tomorrow—even next month or next year—interacting with one another, making plans for future excursions and events. How were they doing that? Sometimes, I could barely see my way forward into the next hour. Next month? Next year? Those were foreign lands that I could not envision.

But over time, the "next-step panic" began to calm. Slowly by slowly, I gained confidence—or at least began to adapt to the new ground beneath my feet. Just as skaters become familiar with the uncertainty of the rolling wheels and the floor moving quickly beneath their feet, I became familiar with the uncertainty of my changing world. As that happened, I gained courage and confidence to lift my head and even, with caution, look toward the future. At the time of this writing, I still find it difficult to go much beyond one year, but that is a world of improvement from when I could not see the next morning.

The ground beneath you has been shaky, uncertain, even dangerous. My hope is that this journey is helping you gain your footing. Perhaps, your eyes are beginning to lift from the ground, even momentarily, to see beyond the next step.

How far can you lift your gaze? Is it painful to look beyond a few days or weeks? Are you beginning to plan for events a month or two down the road? What about next year? Your "distance vision" speaks some truth about your forward movement. Let's talk about it on this bend in the road.

A BEND IN THE ROAD
BEYOND THE NEXT STEP

Use the path below to note some upcoming events. Some might be as simple as a family visit, a dentist appointment, or dinner with friends. Encourage yourself to note something that is approximately six months away, one year away, and perhaps into the trees beyond your sight.

Lifting your eyes, seeing a future for yourself—that is forward movement.

73
PEACE?

"Peace is not the absence of conflict." Have you heard this statement before? Many popular sayings begin with this statement about what peace *is not* and then go on to describe what peace *is*. Let's see if we can come to our own conclusion.

Wouldn't it be lovely if we could create a *peace* that would hover around us like a protective bubble that would keep out all disturbing events and influences? Nice? Yes. Attainable? No. This reality is important for us to keep at the center of our thoughts as we look for peace. Otherwise, we set ourselves up for disappointment and frustration, seeking after a kind of peace that is unattainable for the long term.

This is probably why the opening statement of this chapter is so well-known—because, among other things, the absence of conflict or disturbance is usually unattainable, at least on any long-term basis. This tells us that our peace cannot be connected to *our avoidance of* suffering or conflict or any type of disturbance. Our peace can, however, be connected in some way to *our response* to disturbance.

As I write this, I am speaking to myself. Recently, I have been struggling with anxiety—or with disturbance of my peace—and I have been trying to pin down the source. For now, I am landing on the *what-ifs*.

What if this happens?

What if that person misunderstood my meaning?

What if I can't do this?

What if I am not supposed to do this or that?

You can already see my problem. I am adding to my disturbance by injecting further *possibilities of disturbance*.

The conflict is there. The disturbances are there. The possibilities of further disturbance are there. All these things are all around us. They are unavoidable; therefore, our search for peace cannot depend on ridding our lives of them. Otherwise, we will grasp at peace only to find it repeatedly pulled away.

A few men experienced this situation in a vivid way that provides perfect imagery for us. Jesus and a few of his closest friends were in a boat. The water was calm. The journey was peaceful. Until it wasn't. The water became disturbed, serious waves rose around them, and the what-ifs began:

> What if the boat capsizes?
>
> What if we fall in?
>
> What if we die!

Someone asked the question, "Where is Jesus?" After all, if Jesus was with them, how could this be happening? Where was He?

He was there—in the same boat, in the same storm, experiencing the same disturbance—and He was sleeping peacefully. As the men jostled Him awake, their what-ifs turned to fact, and they told Him, "We are going to drown!"

Jesus called attention to their lack of faith and reassured them, telling them not to be afraid. He then spoke with absolute authority, stilled the threatening waves, and quieted the destructive wind. At His words, all potential for immediate danger ceased. The crisis was over.

It is good that the men knew where to go with their what-ifs. But Jesus showed them there was another possibility—His friends could experience peace *in the midst* of the storm, which included both the disturbance and the what-ifs that seemed to threaten them. But the only way to have such peace was to really understand *who* was in the boat with them.

This story prompts me to make a decisive statement, without maybes, doubts, or apologies:

True peace is only possible when we rest in the ALL *of our Traveling Companion.*

> His "ALL *power*"
>
> His "ALL *presence*"
>
> His "ALL *knowledge*"
>
> His "ALL *goodness*"

Yes, there are times when we can claim peace without Him, but that is usually because we feel some portion of control during those times; for example, maybe we have a back-up plan in place. But true peace, or peace that arises even when we have no control over the situation, can only rise to the surface when two conditions are in place:

- Our minds are filled with the awareness of who God is.
- Our hearts are filled with confidence in His ability to take us safely through the disturbances of this life.

As Isaiah 26:3 in the Bible says, "You will keep in perfect peace those whose minds are steadfast, because they trust in You."

All this leads us to conclude the chapter's opening statement of what peace *is:*

Peace is not the *absence* of conflict . . .
peace is absolute trust in the God who is with us *in that conflict.*

Oh, if only Jesus's friends could have had that absolute trust—they could have remembered who He was and set their minds on Him!

And I, too, should remember. He has proven Himself so many times, and yet, I so often jostle Him, saying, "Where are you? I could go under!" *Jesus is in the boat with me.* He is at peaceful rest, as I should be, and He is the One who speaks with authority to the storm, setting boundaries for my protection. At those times Jesus does as He did with His friends in the boat: He reassures and He reminds of His authority over the storm. Even when our emotions carry us away with panic, He welcomes us to run to Him . . . and jostle Him for attention.

Living in the reality of peace is an intentional decision. What does such a decision look like? Do we simply proclaim, "I *will* have peace!" That seems a bit optimistic—however, there is value when we make an intentional statement of how we are going to live. David, in the midst of danger made a definitive statement of intention in Psalm 4:8:

I *will* lie down and sleep in peace, for You alone, O LORD, make me dwell in safely. (emphasis mine)

But this was not just a strong statement of determination without reason. David's ability to say "I will . . . sleep in peace" was built on the conviction of "for You alone."

The reality is that David's statement of intention is interwoven with the truths he embraced about the object of his peace. Remember that the same was true in our conversation about hope. We discovered that it was not how strongly we hope, but in whom we hope. So, it is not how passionately we proclaim peace to our spirit, but as with David, it is the "for You alone" that makes the peace possible.

Is there possibility for peace? Yes. However, as with hope, we cannot create peace. We can only embrace it—and nurture it. *Only?* These are daunting tasks because emotions and circumstances pull us away from peace and toward anxiousness.

How do we embrace—hold onto—peace?

How do we nurture—feed—peace?

When we believe "for You alone" we choose to follow the instruction given in Philippians 4:6:

Do not be anxious about anything, but in every situation, by prayer and petition, with thanksgiving, present your requests to God.

We choose to not shoulder the burden and huddle waiting for the danger to sweep over us. We talk to our Good Shepherd—freely sharing our fears and concerns. We express gratitude for the evidences of care that we see in our lives. And then we make a choice to wrap ourselves in His assurances, knowing He will be our constant companion.

Let's add another dimension to the feeling and experience of peace. You may be familiar with the Hebrew word, *shalom.* The peace expressed as *shalom* is one of deeply layered meanings. But one expression is the feeling of wholeness, of completeness. *That* is peace—when there is a feeling deep within us that in spite of everything that is happening around us, we are complete, we are whole. There may be chaos in the circumstances of our lives, but we have a sense deep within of "I am okay." As I say, "*Shalom*" to you, I am expressing my desire for you to have a sense of well-being, a feeling of completeness, a feeling of safety. That is truly my hope for you.

What evidence will we see of peace? How will we know if peace is becoming a way of life as we move through suffering toward healing?

The peace of God is mysterious and unexplainable as it settles on us and calms our spirits and our very souls. Peace is also practical and visible as it flows outward onto the pathway of our choices and responses.

At this next bend in the road, we will have the opportunity to think more about the evidence of peace. We will also ponder how to intentionally run after it, embrace it, and live out the mystery.

A BEND IN THE ROAD
EVIDENCE OF PEACE

The time has come to think about the possibility of peace in your life. It can be helpful to name specific moments when you are drawn *away from peace*—and then, consider options that would help *welcome peace* into those moments instead.

Once again, this is a choice that we make. And so, we will think of these as ways to *choose a path of peace.* This goes beyond our healing journey. Every day carries potential for distractions away from peace and into fear and anxiousness—the very emotions that trouble us and distract us from a sense of well-being.

Consider the following possibilities that can open the door for peace in you —emotionally, physically, and spiritually. Connect them to your life and discern times that you go in a contrary direction. Consider ways that this practical path of peace might help you to welcome peace rather than drawing you away toward fear and anxiousness.

How can I choose a path of peace?

- See conflict around me without taking on responsibility to solve that conflict. Not *every* battle is mine to fight.

- Refuse to grasp for "what is not" (to have contentment).

- Set aside the attempt to *control* others, including their actions and responses. I will not spend my energy trying to coerce others to make choices and take actions I see as best.

- Remind myself often of God's provision for me—even in difficult circumstances. I will speak these out-loud as a prayer of gratitude. I will write them on paper so that I can remind of the peace that is possible.

- Accept responsibility for my own actions and responses. Avoid looking for a place to set my *baggage*.

- Respond to the threat of anxiousness from a true awareness of God's love and goodness to me personally. Speak only the truth of assurance rather than accusation or the feeling that He is trying to harm me.

- Set up a boundary to the what-ifs. Give attention to them only long enough to write them on paper—then dispose of them. In a sense, cast them on God.

- Refuse to feed fear so that it grows into panic.

- Put boundaries on things that stir up anxiousness in me. I will avoid movies, television, books, computer research, and such that ignite fear and anxiety and lead me away from peace.

- Nurture—feed—those things that instill and draw me toward a peaceful spirit.

In what other ways can you choose a path of peace?

Above all else, guard your heart, for everything you do flows from it. —
Proverbs 4:23

"Above all else."

Even with all the wisdom and encouragement and instruction our Traveling Companion has given to us, we now hear these words: "Above all else."

He is always thinking of our good.

He knows that we are experiencing healing; He knows that we are gaining courage; and He knows that *we are still vulnerable.* So, He tells us that "Above all else"—meaning *with the utmost determination,* or *ahead of all other defenses*—we should "guard [our] heart." In other words, we should *stay vigilant* or *keep watch* over it. Why? Because everything we do "flows from it."

Take some time to think about what flows from your heart. Loyalty? Love? Mercy? Trust?

It is the heart that most often creates defenses and excuses. It is the heart that most often sees with rose-colored glasses. It is the heart that allows longing to overpower reality. Recklessly, things pour out of our hearts without any careful consideration of the consequences. But God, who is always thinking of our good, says, *"Don't give in so easily! Set some boundaries."*

To guard the heart does not mean that we shut it off, determined not to feel or love. To guard it is to protect it by setting up the kinds of boundaries we discovered earlier—boundaries that guard it from the harm that can come in and the positives that can escape.

But how do we do this?

What boundary, what stronghold, what beautiful protective hedge can guard our hearts?

We nudged opened a door that can reveal this protection in our previous conversation about peace. Remember the practical ways that we can embrace and feed peace from Phillipians 4:6:

> Do not be anxious about anything, but in every situation, by prayer and petition, with thanksgiving, present your requests to God.

And then we discover the answer to our question in the very next verse, Phillipians 4:7:

> And the peace of God which surpasses all understanding,
> will *guard your hearts* and your minds in Christ Jesus (emphasis mine).

The peace of God. This is the very same peace that we discovered in our last conversation. We knew it was necessary and good for us. But now we discover that it also protects our hearts in multiple ways. This peace protects our hearts from feeling doubt, dissatisfaction, and the constant urge to search for something more to "fill the void." It is the search for peace—everywhere but with God—that makes our hearts vulnerable. There is no shortage of things and people and philosophies that promise peace—if only we will . . . However, each promise turns empty after a period of time and we are once again vulnerable to the next intrigue.

Perhaps this is why the peace that God gives—if we embrace it—is *beyond our understanding.* What does that mean? One reason is that it satisfies in a way that nothing else can. There are times that I cannot find the words to adequately express the sense of peace that I have at that moment—perhaps a moment when peace is unexpected. In situations where we might expect to feel frustration, stress, or fear, peace comes as a surprise. It is also true that when we show outward signs of God's peace, it might be beyond the understanding of others—they don't comprehend why we would have peace at such a time.

This peace—God's peace beyond understanding—*is what is needed to protect my heart.*

That choice to trust the perfect provider of peace—and embrace that peace—is what then guards your heart, for your good. You do not need to go looking for other escapes or defenses. Your heart is not in turmoil. Your heart is not drawn towards other protectors. Your heart is centered on *"You alone"* who protects it from all dangers and potential for crises—those you can see—and those you cannot.

You cannot create peace, for it is a unique sense of calm that God creates, but you can embrace it, allow it to take root, nurture it, and live into it. And as the peace settles around your heart, you will discover that you are protected and strengthened.

A BEND IN THE ROAD
GUARDING MY HEART
WITH PEACE

Contemplate the following questions and write your responses in the space that follows.

- What tendencies of my heart are weak and often get me into harmful situations?

- How could the peace of God protect me from wandering into dangerous situations?

- What keeps me from embracing this "peace beyond understanding?"

HOW DO WE NOW LIVE?

Do you remember when we began this contemplative journey? When the first few bends in the road caused us to stop and contemplate our time of suffering? We opened boxes that were closed. We spoke honestly to ourselves and expressed emotions—some expected and others, perhaps, a surprise. Little by little, we made our way through suffering until, eventually, we found that we could turn our faces toward healing.

Now, we are here. *All* is not resolved, but we have gained more clarity. Suffering is not *gone*, but we have become familiar with it enough to deflect some of its sting, to weaken its intimidation and control. This means we have reached a particularly important place on our journey: that point where we can think about the path beyond.

We have already discussed some of what to expect on that future path, and how to prepare accordingly. We know now how to create healthy boundaries and how to rethink our vocabulary; we forsee the likelihood that we will stumble, but we have the capacity to get back on track when we do; we are even discovering how to embrace the real possibility that peace may now enter the picture.

And yet, as we begin to courageously raise our eyes from the ground under our feet to more distant points on the road, it's as if something else is there, in the periphery. Something that gives us pause and feels threatening to our forward movement. What is it?

If we retraced our steps, we would find that it has been furtively hovering in our thoughts. From the moment the awareness of our pain settled in, the vulnerability for further pain also took up residence. Now as we have opened our hearts, our minds—our very souls—to peace and hope, we are swiftly reminded how those treasures can be—have been—stolen . . . by suffering.

And there it is. We have found the "something else" in our periphery: it is that likelihood that we'll meet more suffering down the road.

From the outset, our goal on this journey was to find our way *out* of the negative effects of suffering. And we have! As a part of that process, though, we spoke much about the pain and trauma of our past—and this discussion revealed to us the reality of *suffering in the present* and the *likelihood of suffering to come.*

So, although it may seem strange, our arrival at this place where we can see the potential for peace came through our awareness of suffering:

> suffering in our past,
> suffering in the present, and
> suffering yet to come.

This paradox is unavoidable; it comes from our *knowledge of good and evil.*

It harkens back to the story of our very creation—back to the beautiful, perfect garden where humankind first lived, full of newness and goodness, until they ate from the forbidden tree of the knowledge of good and evil. It was then that sin entered the scene; and as a natural consequence of their newfound knowledge, so did suffering.

Now, suffering is a natural part of the picture—an integral part of our path here on earth. Muddy roads. Potholes. Threats of crisis. Uncertain times.

And so, as we arrive at this place where we want to begin courageously looking outward, at this point where we sense the threat of future pain hovering over the potential for peace, how do we live? How do we live in a way that we will not be blindly vulnerable to future suffering? How do we live in a way that we will not give in to despair when more pain crosses our path? Knowing all that we now know about suffering and ourselves, *how do we now live?*

There is no formula to follow to answer that question. Rather, the truths that we have absorbed often will naturally sway us toward new responses, which will then build upon one another to create life anew. However, there is one perspective that might nudge us closer to a reply that we can be at peace with.

A NEW PERSPECTIVE

To go forward from this place, we need a firm foundation upon which we can piece together our new building blocks of awareness; a platform on which we can weave our awareness of good and evil together with our awareness of truth, to create a rich tapestry of courage and peace. How do we now live?

- We expect suffering and acknowledge the good in it. By doing this, we neutralize some of the threats that hold us in fear.
- We embrace suffering and come to peace with the pain. By doing this, we calm the intensity of the battle that drains us.
- We acknowledge God by our side in healing and embrace God in our suffering. By doing this, we discover a source of strength and value, and an assurance of a future.

But understanding these ideas about our relationship with suffering is only the beginning of this perspective. There is more.

Let's go back for a moment to that beautiful, perfect garden. Everything was as it was intended to be; there was no fear and no sorrow. What a delightful place to spend our days!

Now, fast forward . . . You may or may not know that there is coming a time when God will once again make all things new and perfect and beautiful. He tells us this in his Word:

> See, I will create a new heavens and a new earth. The former things will not be remembered, nor will they come to mind. Isaiah 65:17

> He will wipe every tear from their eyes. There will be no more death or mourning or crying or pain, for the old order of things has passed away. He who was seated on the throne said, "I am making everything new!" (Revelation 21:4-5)

These verses describe a time of newness when fear and sorrow will be wiped away—no longer will they threaten our peace. What a wonderful promise for the future.

Until that time, however, we physically live in this broken world "between." Let's look at a visual example of this "between" place.

Perhaps, you have always envisioned your life in this way:

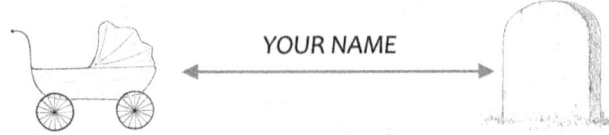

YOUR NAME

The truth is that we do not exist *only* in this place between; there is *more* to this life. There was a time *before*, when God conceived each of us in His mind; and there will be a time *after*, when we can live forever with the One who created us and who loves us for all eternity.

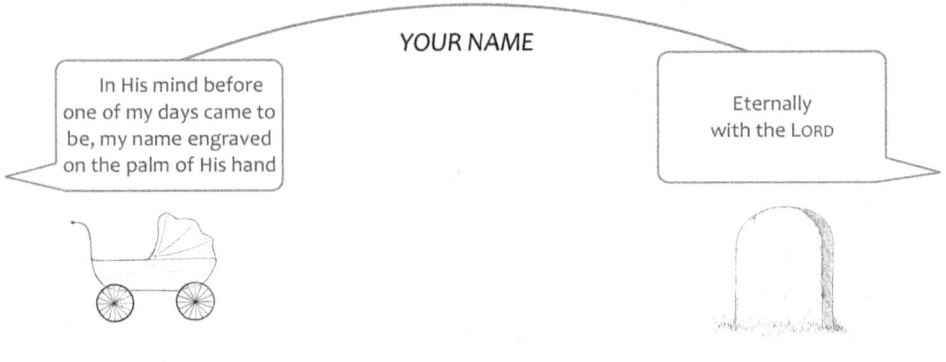

YOUR NAME

In His mind before one of my days came to be, my name engraved on the palm of His hand

Eternally with the LORD

Your eyes saw my unformed body; all the days ordained for me were written in your book before one of them came to be. (Psalm 139:16)

I give them eternal life, and they shall never perish; no one will snatch them out of my hand. (John 10:28)

THINGS ABOVE

Our Good God wants us to remember this perspective that our existence is so much more than the "between." He wants this for us because He knows that such a perspective helps us come to peace with *all* of the events on our journey, past, present, and future—this includes the pain, the joy, and even the unexpected. Colossians 3:2–3 puts it this way: "Set your minds on things above, not on earthly things. For . . . your life is now hidden with Christ in God."

When we set our minds "on things above," or on the eternal, we find that we are no longer tied to this "between" time—and that can give us a whole new viewpoint on suffering and on life in general.

Let's talk about this redeemed view of suffering, along with a few others that come with an eternal perspective:

Our suffering is temporary. **Suffering exists only on earth, in this "between" part of our lives. And because this part of our lives is temporary, so, too, is suffering.**

We find a sense of purpose, hope, and joy beyond this world. **Let's remember Jesus's example, who** "for the *joy* set before him . . . endured the cross" (Hebrews 12:2; emphasis mine). **Jesus knew that not only was** *His suffering temporary* **but that** *His purpose extended far beyond* **a single moment in time. He also had** *hope*—for *the joy that lay beyond the immediate pain.*

Jesus wants us to have this same perception of time as being "beyond," because He knows from experience that it is what will carry us through the difficulties of the present world toward the dependable hope (not wish) of the eternal joy to come.

We find a sense of value and safety beyond this world. **This world was never meant to be a place of definitive answers or a settled sense of home. This means that we are not obligated to "get it all right," as if the events of this life define us for all time or are our only chance for happiness.**

This life is an opportunity. When we walk through this "between" time with Jesus, His light shines through us. This gives us the opportunity to express the image of God, by reflecting His eternal light into the temporary darkness.

> Therefore . . . we do not lose heart. . . . For God, who said, "Let light shine out of darkness," has shone in our hearts to give the light of the knowledge of the glory of God in the face of Jesus Christ. (2 Corinthians 4:1, 6)

Again, shining God's light does not require us to "get it all right." It simply means remembering God is with us and embracing hope, even as we live with the awareness of suffering:

> We have this treasure in jars of clay to show that this all-surpassing power is from God and not from us. We are hard pressed on every side, but not crushed; perplexed, but not in despair; persecuted, but not abandoned; struck down, but not destroyed. (2 Corinthians 4:7–9)

This life is preparation. This life is intended to be a time of growing in familiarity and connection to Jesus, to prepare for our time with Him in eternity.

SO, HOW DO WE NOW LIVE?

Now that we have talked about what it means to have an eternal perspective, let's remember our original question: As we arrive at this place where we want to courageously look toward peace but fear the potential for more suffering down the road, *how do we now live?*

We now live knowing that while life is here and now, it also stretches beyond the boundaries of our current world. This gives us a healthy view of suffering, one in which we move ever forward with courage and peace, because we embrace the mysteries of hope, peace, an eternal identity, and a God who is always with us—both in the "between" and in the "beyond."

EMBRACING THE "BEYOND" MYSTERIES

An eternal vantagepoint enables us to understand truths about the bigger picture of our lives, putting the role of suffering in proper perspective. Our lives "beyond" include the time before we are born; the time we are living now, in this temporary world; and the time in our future when we will live with God in eternity.

The time before we are born gives us courage. We are sure about and mindful of our value, as God conceived of us in thought before we ever came to be. We can move forward on the road in confidence and courage because we know we were created in the image of God, who is good and who was there in the beginning.

The time we are living now gives us a full awareness of God's role in suffering. We remain fully aware of the suffering and pain in this temporary present life, while also becoming fully aware that God, who is good, is here.

The future time of eternity gives us hope. We are convinced of and focused on the hope for a redeemed and perfect eternal home, where suffering will cease, and we know that God, who is good, is there.

EMBRACING THE "BETWEEN" MYSTERIES

Let's expand on "the time we are living now," which is this "between" time. When we take on an eternal perspective, we can embrace these particular mysteries about our temporary lives on this earth:

This world is broken and we suffer, but the Spirit of God is more powerful—and He is always with us. We are journeying together in this broken world that touches us often with its mud and grime. Evil infects it, entering our lives through people and influences. And suffering is the result. But beside us the whole time is a Traveling Companion who is more powerful than any suffering we encounter.

We acknowledge the muddy road, the storm clouds—along with the shade trees, the rays of sun, the new green of growth.

God gives us glimpses of beauty in this world, in proportion to the pain. Not only is this Traveling Companion always by our side; He is good and caring enough to give us glimpses of beauty in proportion to the pain.

The truth is, although this world is broken, it continues to carry the imprint of God's creative hand, because the beauty and glory of His creation cannot be destroyed. And so, whether in full view or waiting to be discovered, it makes itself known to us. We see it in nature, in music, in art, in science, and in fellow image-bearers of the Creator.

God's beauty is all around us. And its presence in this world is an expression of His love, grace, and mercy toward us.

In this time between, we often expect (or, at least, we are not surprised by) suffering. But we now know that we can look for and draw attention to God's beauty and Spirit—to His power, love, grace, and mercy— even during our times of pain. This makes us more willing to remain open to suffering's arrival; it assures us that, no matter the struggle, our companion will be there, and we will be ready to absorb whatever He has to offer. And the more we release the push-back we feel against suffering —whether present or potential—and the more we absorb His healing, the more able we will be to become conduits of His beauty and healing to others.

Over time, as we continue to embrace this eternal perspective, we will find the tapestry of our story growing in a beautiful, complex, and expressive way that could only be made possible as suffering and healing intertwine.

Perhaps, the notes of pain and healing will even blend to create the beginning of a new melody—only a few notes at first, that play quietly in our mind. But eventually, as we learn to open our hearts wider, to lift our eyes higher, we are sure to discover the presence of a new song.

A BEND IN THE ROAD
STEPS FORWARD

How do I respond to the eternal nature of my existence—the before and the after? How does this truth help "life" come into perspective?

How will I now live in a way that is different from before?

Is it possible for me to see—look for—beauty intertwined with suffering?

JOY AND MUSIC

At first glance,
joy seems to betray the suffering.
But, do not be afraid of the
melody that is beginning.
It is part of your new song.

You have turned my wailing into dancing; you removed my sackcloth and clothed me with joy, that my heart may sing your praises and not be silent. Lord my God, I will praise you forever. —Psalm 30:11–12

This is what we long for, isn't it?

At first glance, joy seems to betray the suffering. We are unsure if it fits into the narrative. We hold it at arm's length.

As if allowing it in could jeopardize the true telling of our story. As if expressing it could nullify the contradictory ache.

So, does joy make light of the pain? Or does it imply that everything is "fixed?"

Joy is unique. Different from happiness, it is not dependent on circumstances. And so, yes, it belongs in our narrative. Even in those who have suffered, there is evidence of joy: it is the golden thread woven into the multicolored tapestry that tells our story.

In a life of suffering, joy is evidence of . . .

a soul that has been wounded but is not crushed.

a spirit that has been perplexed but is not in despair.

a body that has been struck down but is not destroyed.

One synonym for *joy* is *wonder*, once again suggesting mystery—something unexplainable, yet undeniable. This comes as no surprise, since joy arrives most often when I feel the wonder of God's care. At times, I have experienced His intimate provision: a gift that meets a personal need still unvoiced deep within—sometimes, a need I had not even recognized!

In those times, I open my arms and embrace the profound mystery that He is present with me, and *joy* washes over me.

And then we discover that joy does not travel alone.

The book of Nehemiah tells us about a time when God's people were disconsolate. Ezra was reading the law of Moses to them and they were undone—weeping because of past events in their own lives and the lives of their ancestors. Then Nehemiah speaks clearly and tells them to stop grieving because:

> "... the joy of the LORD is your strength" (Nehemiah 8:10).

Joy has a traveling companion—*strength*.

Think about it. We all know the weariness of depression. Exhaustion, listlessness—emotional and physical fatigue flourish when we are downhearted and anxious. "Be strong!" people say. Yet, strength seems evasive and out of reach. Where do we find strength when we are undone?

Strength grows and flourishes in the presence of joy.

- We look for God's care and provision. We rejoice with gratitude.
- We open our eyes to beauty. We allow it to penetrate our heart.
- We enlarge our perspective to see our value and purpose beyond this "between" life with its muddy roads.
- We smile to acknowledge "I AM" on the journey with us.

We may not be able to suddenly leap mountains in a single bound—but we will find that we can accomplish that one difficult task facing us on the day. And as we feed the joy, we will grow stronger.

Joy is open to all of us. But, as we have learned along our journey, we alone can choose to embrace the moments of healing we are offered. This includes the choice to accept joy.

To be without it is a loss—an empty place that is *felt*.

Do not be afraid of joy. Your joy is not a betrayal of the suffering. Joy is part of your new song.

A BEND IN THE ROAD
EXPRESSIONS OF JOY

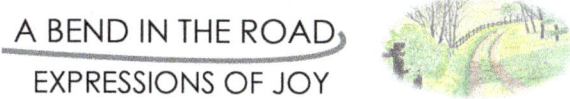

This bend in the road is an opportunity to express joy. To acknowledge and embrace it.

We will stop here now for a bit. But you will likely return to this bend, because joy comes along the journey unexpectedly, in moments of wonder that remind us:

> We are valuable.

> We have purpose.

> We are not consumed.

Record these moments — they are treasures to be kept and pondered.

YOUR NEW SONG

I can hear it. As I sit writing, I can hear the notes, the melodies, the phrases—expressing hope, value, identity. Your song is being heard, even if you are not fully aware of it yet.

I have tried to visualize when I first became aware of my new song. There may have been moments that slipped past me; but I clearly remember a particular time. In the early days of my crisis, I needed to make life-changing choices. The task of disposing of my belongings and leaving my home to find an apartment was difficult and disorienting. My Good Shepherd prepared each step and held my hand as I numbly attempted to follow. He provided a sweet little apartment with a backdrop of trees.

As I sat on my second-floor balcony, with thoughts scrambled and emotions in a tangled mess, my ears picked up the notes of a precious visitor. My vision focused and there he was on the tippy top of the tree intent on gaining my attention.

As I released myself into that moment and gave myself permission to experience beauty . . . I began to hear music once again. My visitor came back multiple times (I was able to capture this picture), and I knew this was one of those precious and personal gifts from my Good Shepherd, a memorable bend in the road of my healing.

I do not know when your awareness will come. Perhaps you are already hearing the notes. The melody will be different from the one you used to sing. It will come from deep within, rooted in the soil of suffering. It will rise out of the pain. It might carry an expression of your gratitude to God that He is with you in your suffering. That He heard your cry. That He set your feet on a rock. Maybe the song is just beginning with the awareness that you have not been consumed and that there is beauty in your story.

But your new song is your own. No two songs sound alike. The melody is part of your story; it came to life before you were born and it will continue into eternity. Don't be afraid to let it flow from you—a few notes or a full oratorio! Don't worry about what others think or say. After all, you are singing your new song to your trusted Traveling Companion, your Good Shepherd, your Savior, your I Am:

Sing to the Lord a new song; sing to the Lord . . . (Psalm 96:1)

I have struggled with how to bring this to a close. I suppose the truth is that I don't want to end our conversation. And so . . . I will see you along the journey. I have confidence that we are moving forward, slowly by slowly. Perhaps, at some point, we'll stop at the same bend in the road.

We will know each other by our voices, as we lift them together, making beautiful music that resonates with courage and peace.

Can you hear it?

Your path is unique.
Take time to ponder the blessings
and the challenges . . .
the joy and the suffering . . .
the bright hues and the dark shades.
Avoid not one bend in the road.
All weave the exquisite tapestry of your life
with perfect design.

INVITATION TO RESPOND

After several years of writing and pondering over *A New Song,* I found that the book became part of me. It took up residence in my mind, sometimes sitting on the periphery and other times consuming my thoughts and demanding attention. In some of my writing sessions, words just poured out and fell into place on the page; in others, I struggled for hours to find one illusive phrase that would express my thoughts. But through all of it, I knew there would come a time when I had to say, "It's complete." At that moment, there would be no more explanation, no more clarification. I would simply have to hand it off to you, the reader, with the hope that you'd understand and receive my intentions well.

When I eventually reached that point, I realized that one thing I could do is offer you an opportunity to respond. And now, that is what I am inviting you to do.

You are welcome to share words, a thought, a drawing. Perhaps, you want to share your response to one of the bends in the road or a way you gained courage or peace. Maybe you want to tell about a struggle that still remains.

There is no form or template to fill out. Simply reach out to me via email, at susan@susanhabeggerauthor.com, or through the "Contact Me" option at susanhabeggerauthor.com.

Finally, if *A New Song* was helpful to you, I would appreciate a short review on Amazon.com, so that other readers might benefit from your words and from this book.

AVAILABLE NOW: *A NEW SONG LEADER'S GUIDE* FOR SMALL GROUP STUDY

Why Use *A New Song* For A Group Study?

As the writing of *A New Song* neared completion, it was read and used by pre-release small groups, and the response was remarkable. It brought to light the number of people who need a defined way to begin the conversation about hurt and healing—particularly in the church, where it seems this discussion is often set aside.

This avoidance by the church could happen for a variety of reasons:

- Maybe we assume people don't want to talk about or listen to personal problems as a part of their everyday conversations.
- Maybe we are afraid of what will be shared.
- Maybe we think these types of conversations should be reserved for professional counseling.
- Maybe we fear such discussions will detract from the positive messages we believe should be given in church.

Regardless of the reasons, many shared that they generally feel the absence of this type of conversation in the church. It is as if there is an unspoken expectation that our experiences of suffering are to be kept outside the doors of worship. There is the offer—and even the expectation—of healing, but aside from the random counseling referral, there is often little to no guidance in how to get there. There is no provision of a safe time and space where we can talk openly about the raw, unfiltered hurt that we need healing for.

This is where *A New Song* comes in. Innately built into this book for individuals going through suffering is a format that churches can work within to conduct safe, relevant, and organized conversations around this difficult topic.

And that's just what this book study is—*a conversation*. It is *not* a counseling course and should not be offered as group therapy. The author of the book is not a licensed counselor and, most likely, neither are the leaders who will facilitate the small-group discussions. Rather, it is a safe, organized, intentional opportunity for people to talk openly and productively about their experiences of suffering and their responses to the disappointments, loss, and trauma in their lives.

Along those lines, perhaps the main benefit of applying *A New Song* to a small-group study is that it provides guidance for that discussion—and in a group where people are faced with becoming vulnerable through sharing, this guidance provides a welcome safety net. Let me give you a couple examples.

Imagine starting a small group for sharing pain and then simply "winging it." The results could be disastrous and do more harm than good. All of us long to share our stories, including our painful ones, but without any guidance for this process, we often struggle. What should we share? And how much? How do we "deliver" our story? Often, we either share too much and feel uncomfortable because we can't move forward, or we close ourselves off, putting on the face we think others expect to see—the one that says, "Yes, I have problems, but I have everything under control." Then, once pain is shared, we wonder what to do with it. How do we respond? Do we become a dumping ground for emotion? Do we make a list of ways to "set things right?" By providing guidance for this part of the journey, *A New Song* gives participants and leaders a space in which they can feel freedom to engage in safe, relevant sharing—and ultimately, to grow.

The guidance itself is neither a dictated path, with a checklist to mark our progress, nor a free-for-all, inviting everyone to share from whatever topic they choose. It does not promise a quick fix to people's problems. It also does not begin with the answer and then encourage people to fit their problems into that answer. Rather, the guidance in *A New Song* begins with the person. It allows individuals to give attention to their unique experiences of pain without accusation or expectation, and then gently lays down steppingstones of truth that pave a path toward healing—principles they can use to discover how to come to peace with the suffering of their past, present, and future.

In the group setting, the natural outgrowth of this focus on the person is the nurtured bond between people. There is the recognition that each person is on a unique journey. We know that group members will not face the same situations, feel the same emotions, or make the same choices—

but they will have an opportunity to discover and embrace the similarities they encounter as they travel parts of the road together. And as they share the journey and are guided toward a common focus, their sense of companionship and togetherness will grow.

Finally, using *A New Song* in a small-group book study can further the opportunity for ministry. Sometimes, as believers, we hesitate to reveal the rawness of our pain and suffering. We feel the church should exemplify life at its fullest, presenting the image that "all is well." But perhaps, it is by our acknowledgment that all is *not* well that we open the door to an awareness of peace, courage, and moments of healing—and arrive at a place where we discover what it *means* for all to be well. It could be that, through this very openness to pain, we become true examples of what it looks like to live life at its fullest. And it is only this real and truthful journey toward healing that gives the opportunity for the display of God's provision and love, since it is He who journeys with us and helps us.

We don't need to be afraid to talk about suffering. It is one of our most common experiences. Our stories long to be told, and our hearts cry out to be heard. Our spirits yearn for the permission to express disquiet—followed by the gentle reminder that we have a reason for hope.

My desire, then, is that *A New Song* will provide church communities with . . .

- the encouragement to speak about pain openly and without fear;
- the foothold and assistance they need to come alongside those who long for a safe place—and companionship—to travel the path toward healing;
- the opportunity to introduce those experiencing pain to The Good Shepherd, our perfect Traveling Companion.

My hope is that, together, we can live out the following reality and help others to do the same:

> He put a new song in my mouth,
> a hymn of praise to our God.
> *Many will see* and fear the LORD
> *and put their trust in him.*
> —Psalm 40:3, emphasis mine

ABOUT THE AUTHOR

Susan Habegger, founder and director of Thrive Life Skills, an international ministry organization, has lived and worked for over 30 years with suffering people around the world, but not until she unexpectedly met suffering firsthand did her thoughts on healing transform, inspiring her to write *A New Song*. Susan lives with her daughter and family in Michigan, where she explores the Lake Michigan shores. Her constant companion, at home or traveing, is her Good Shepherd.

The conversations in *A New Song* are excellent topics for Conferences, Workshops, and Retreats. To request Susan as speaker, go to susanhabeggerauthor.com for more information.